100 LOCALS IN LONDON

Reveal their favorite restaurants,
coffee bars, and secret spots

LONDON

LONDON

100 Locals in London
Reveal their favorite restaurants, pubs, and secret spots

Copyright © 2025 Mavenhill

Mavenhill and its emblem are registered trademarks

ISBN: 978-1-940387-18-5

www.onehundredlocals.com

100 LOCALS IN LONDON

Reveal their favorite restaurants,
pubs, and secret spots

DON'T BE A TOURIST, BE A LONDONER

We live in a world where every product or service you might want to purchase has already been reviewed online by thousands of satisfied and frustrated clients alike. From the local coffee shop to your next electric car, our consumer decisions have never been better informed. Yet, when it comes to travel and leisure in foreign destinations, there is often a huge knowledge gap about how the locals live and play.

In a city like London, renowned for its sprawling parks, vibrant culinary diversity, and unrivaled pub culture, do you really want to follow the Instagram herds to the same predictable places? To queue endlessly at overrated landmarks, eat uninspired fish and chips at touristy traps, or pay triple for a lackluster pint at a pub where no Londoner would set foot?

In this crowd-sourced guide to the metropolis, 100 Londoners share their secret spots, their top restaurants, and their favorite pubs. Savvy travelers might already know a few of these recommendations, but most will be delightful surprises you'll struggle to find on the usual "trip advisory" sites. Even ChatGPT and its other AI counterparts (yes, you too, Gemini) don't have access to this carefully curated dataset. Brimming with analog suggestions of where to relax, dine, and drink, this guide invites you to explore London's neighborhoods and uncover the best-kept secrets of a city loved fiercely by its locals.

Londoners adore their city. They thrive on its eclectic energy, savor its ever-changing dining scene, and embrace the slower pace of life when needed—whether lounging in a centuries-old pub or wandering along the Thames at sunset. This book is as much a travel guide as it is a love letter to a city brimming with life, resilience, and constant reinvention.

Whether you're a seasoned visitor, a first-timer, or even a born-and-bred Londoner, prepare to discover this endlessly fascinating city in its truest hues. Hues as captivating as the warm glow of its historic streetlamps illuminating cobblestone alleys and the shimmering reflections of its iconic landmarks on the river.

In this new edition, we introduce a fresh roster of cool Londoners, capturing the city's evolving culinary and cultural tastes. While there are plenty of hot new favorites, many timeless establishments made the list effortlessly. Take The George Inn on Borough High Street, for instance—a pub with roots stretching back to the 17th century. It's not going anywhere.

Contents

100 Locals in London
— *Reveal their local secrets*

Credits
— *Who made me?*

Editor - *Maven Hill*
Design - *Joe Scerri*
Interviews - *Genevieve Joy,*
Catherine Baumgartner
Photography - *Benjamin South,*
Amr Nabeel, Alessio Cesario,
Jerome Dominici, Alfcermed,
David Peterson, Andrea De Santis,
and Alex Hill.

Map - *Free Vector Maps*

© 2025 Mavenhill

Special thanks to:
The City of London

Trafalgar Square,
London, 6.40 am

My secret to happiness:

"Don't try too hard. Everything will come. In the meantime, enjoy life."

Karin C. Bauer

Personal Trainer

— *Born in Dubai, now based in London, recommends...*

Made or Born Londoner?

> *I was born in Dubai, moved to Germany and eventually London to study."*

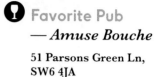

🔓 Secret Spot
— *Chelsea Farmers Market*

This farmers market in the heart of Chelsea every Saturday is foodie heaven. Whether you're craving exciting street grub, looking to fill your fridge with delectable cheeses, eager to pick up some artisanal breads, or even keen to try some champagne with high-end oysters, this market never disappoints. And it's right next to the Saatchi Gallery, which is always a treat to visit.

🏆 Favorite Pub
— *Amuse Bouche*

51 Parsons Green Ln, SW6 4JA

I prefer champagne bars. Also in Fulham, this is the perfect place for cocktails before starting the night or unwinding with my girlfriends. It's great on Thursdays and absolutely amazing on Fridays. Pubs in London are like cafés in Rome – it's almost impossible to find a bad one. Finding a bad pub is harder than finding a unicorn.

🍴 Favorite Restaurant
— *Boys'N'Berry*

839 Fulham Rd., SW6 5HQ

This is one of my favorite brunch spots in the heart of trendy Fulham, a short walk away from Parsons Green tube station. The decor is really trendy and urban, with exposed brick walls, etc. They don't take reservations but have a seating area downstairs. I've been there a few times during peak hours over the weekend, and my friends and I were always accommodated. The staff is simply lovely, beaming with smiles and care. Being a personal trainer, when I eat out, I pick places that use fresh, healthy, and real ingredients without compromising on taste! Their halloumi omelette will have you coming back for more. I also highly recommend the salmon and sweet potato mash. Being part Italian originally, coffee is sacrosanct for me, and they nail that too.

What do you like most about living in London?

> *There is always something to do in this city. People always ask me if I ever get bored from the noise and the crowds, and my answer is always no. I can wake up one day and decide, today I'd like to go to the cinema or see a show in the West End. There are plenty of green spaces and opportunities to do outdoor activities. London has something for everyone."*

Favorite Restaurant
— *Boys'N'Berry*

My secret to happiness:

"My grandchildren, and to drink the best wine and eat the best food."

Jeffrey William Cadge

Florist

— Born in South London, recommends...

Made or Born a Londoner?

> *I was born in Bermondsey in South London and have lived my entire life in this city. I used to work in printing until Mr. Murdoch killed that industry."*

🔒 Secret Spot
— *St. Lukes Gardens*

Tucked away in the heart of Chelsea, off the bustling King's Road, this garden complex is an oasis of relaxation. Whenever I'm on a break or have some free time, I slip in there with a book and a sandwich and lose myself in the serenity. On the same grounds is a beautiful 19th-century Gothic-style church where Charles Dickens was married in 1836. If you are a fan of his work, you must visit.

🍷 Favorite Pub
— *The Cadogan Arms*

298 King's Rd, SW3 5UG

A long-standing pub in the heart of Chelsea that has changed ownership a few times. The newest owners have renovated it tastefully while maintaining the spirit of the original place. Amazing gastro pub food, including the best fish and chips ever, glazed duck, and of course, roasts. Sets the gold standard.

🍴 Favorite Restaurant
— *Ziani*

45 Radnor Walk, SW3 4BP

Right off the King's Road in Chelsea, this family-run Italian restaurant is iconic and one of my favorites in London. The chef and owner is Roberto, and you can see him preparing the food with love. It's where I take my wife on the most special occasions like anniversaries, as well as friends and family. The atmosphere is extremely relaxed and homey, and unlike many places in London, the prices for a meal out are very reasonable. The way they prepare scallops slightly seared with a side of wild mushrooms and a rocket salad with shaved Parmigiano just makes my mouth water thinking about it. I also love the rack of lamb. Needless to say, their desserts and wine list are superb.

What do you like most about living in London?

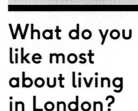

> *I love the hard-working people of London like me, or what you would call the Cockneys. They're the best in the world and will give you their heart, body and soul if you are ever in trouble. They're the real spirit of this city and they provide the color, the humor, the life, and soul that makes London what it is. I also love the nightlife and the spirit of the city. By day, we work hard, and when we're done, we know how to have fun and enjoy ourselves."*

Made or Born a Londoner?

> *I was born in Hampstead, then moved to Buckinghamshire when I was a young boy, but eventually found my way back to London twenty-five years ago, and it's been home since."*

🍴 Favorite Restaurant
— *Langan's Brasserie*

Stratton St, W1J 8LB

In the Green Park neighborhood of central London, this iconic French restaurant is best known for once being owned by the British actor, Sir Michael Caine. While it primarily serves French cuisine, it's also one of the best places for a Sunday roast. Despite being a favorite hangout for celebrities, it offers a mid-range dining experience in terms of price. It's known for its art collection, featuring works by David Hockney, Lucian Freud, and others. This place is an institution, and a visit to London wouldn't be complete without dining there!

My secret to happiness:

"A good bottle of wine."

Scott Norveil

Actor

— Born and bred in London recommends...

Secret Spot 🔒
— *Battersea Park*

Battersea Park is a serene oasis in bustling London, my secret gem. It offers a perfect blend of nature and art, with stunning gardens, a picturesque lake, and intriguing sculptures. Ideal for peaceful walks or picnics, it's a place where you can escape the city's frenzy and immerse yourself in tranquility. Its hidden treasures, like the Peace Pagoda, add a unique charm that's hard to find elsewhere in London.

🍸 Favorite Pub
— *Kings Arms Chelsea*

190 Fulham Rd., SW10 9PN

A pub serves many roles for me. As someone self-employed in the creative industries, it's the ideal spot to set up my laptop, dive into my zone, and work on my writing projects. But it's also where I connect with friends—to hang out, unwind, celebrate, watch a game, and everything in between. Plus, the food here is incredibly good.

What do you love most about London?

> *That I could never leave it. I'm captivated by its creativity and global diversity—it's almost like a country within a country."*

Favorite
Restaurant
—*Antepliler*

Made or Born a Londoner?

" I grew up in East London, in a suburb called East Ham. It was totally gentrified after the Olympics; I hardly recognize it. Now I live in Manor House near Haringay in North London."

" The fact that you can traverse London from end to end in half an hour and find yourself in a completely different world is truly remarkable. While most visitors flock to the glamorous neighborhoods like Chelsea, known for their affluence, these areas can sometimes feel a bit dull. In contrast, Manor House, where I live, is vibrant and bursting with multicultural goodness. I cherish the diversity within the same city.

What do you like most about living in London?

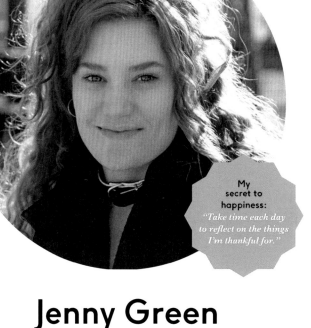

My secret to happiness: *"Take time each day to reflect on the things I'm thankful for."*

Jenny Green

Makeup Artist

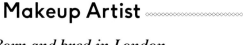

— Born and bred in London, recommends...

 ## Favorite Restaurant
— Antepliler

45-46 Grand Parade, Green Lanes, N4 1AG

This is a small and affordable restaurant in the ethnically diverse and very hip Green Lanes strip in Harringay. They have three different establishments: a café and tea house; a pâtisserie offering baklava, house-made ice creams, and other sweet delights, and the main restaurant. You get free hummus, salad, and bread. I usually go for a veggie dish, so it's perfect for vegetarians and vegans. They make amazing things with aubergines. My carnivorous friends who I've taken there tell me the kebabs and grilled meats are cooked to perfection.

 ## Secret Spot
— Lee Valley White Water Centre

Located in a hidden part of Hackney, this secret spot offers open swimming in summer and other water activities like kayaking and rafting. Not widely known, it's perfect for escaping the city. The water is crystal clear. The closest train station is Waltham Cross.

Favorite Pub
— The Faltering Fullback

19 Perth Rd, N4 3HB

This Irish pub is in Finsbury Park and has an incredible four-tiered Babylon-style garden, heated during winter. While primarily known as a rugby pub, it offers much more. Enjoy live music, including Irish fiddle bands, which are always highly entertaining. Don't miss out on their delicious Thai menu.

My secret to happiness:

"Finding time to do the things that I love doing."

Stacey Gledhill

Painter

— *Born in New Zealand and adopted by London, recommends...*

Made or Born Londoner?

❝ *Born in Wellington, New Zealand, I ventured to London years ago to embark on my career journey."*

🔒 Secret Spot
— *Hampstead Heath*

This park is a part of the city that makes you feel like you are somewhere else. Like you've left the throbbing metropolis and have been transported to an oasis of tranquility and natural beauty. It's London's sanctuary, where time slows amid sprawling greenery. Its wild charm whispers tales of Keats and Constable. Ponds beckon for tranquil reflection; hills offer city panoramas.

🏆 Favorite Pub
— *Southampton Arms*

139 Highgate Rd, NW5 1LE

This quaint pub nestled in Kentish Town exudes charm with its old-school vibe. Though once cash-only, it maintains its nostalgic atmosphere even with credit card acceptance. Offering an impressive array of ales, beers, and lagers, it's the perfect spot for a laid-back Sunday, complete with live piano, ideal for catching up with friends.

🍴 Favorite Restaurant
— *Rosa's Thai Brixton*

36 Atlantic Rd, SW9 7DG

Nestled in vibrant Brixton Market, this charming Thai eatery exudes a cozy, intimate vibe, reminiscent of dining in someone's kitchen. Their Phad Thai, both classic and inventive, is my go-to comfort dish, while the seafood platter, featuring exquisite calamari, prawns, and seabass, is pure heaven.

What do you like most about living in London?

❝ *London embodies incredible freedom. Arriving here with my twin sister, we sought a departure from our upbringing. In this melting pot of dreams, everyone pursues their own aspirations, yet relishes life's moments. Amidst the hustle, it's not a city that overwhelms; rather, it empowers."*

Secret Spot
— *Victoria Embankment Gardens*

Right by the Embankment station, this quaint little park is never busy and is a slice of paradise in the middle of the big crazy city. In summer, you can take your towel and a good book and bask in the sun. There is a small café for light all-day food and ice cream.

 ## Favorite Pub
— *Trinity Arms*

45 Trinity Gardens, SW9 8DR

This pub in Brixton has been recently refurbished. The bar is right in the middle, and there are pockets of seating areas around which makes the flow amazing whether you want to chill or mingle. It's lively and inevitably the only pub I find myself going to.

My secret to happiness:

"Good food, and then some more."

Made or Born Londoner?

66 *I was born in Guildford, Surrey, which is half an hour away from London. I moved here for work."*

Sophie Wood
Branding Specialist

— *Born and bred in London, recommends...*

What do you like most about living in London?

66 *I love that London is a cultural melting pot. You can step out onto the street and meet people from all corners of the world. Professionally, it's also one of the best places to work and make a career in whatever industry you are in."*

 ## Favorite Restaurant
— *Mildreds*

9 Jamestown Rd, NW1 7BW

This vegan restaurant in Camden is my absolute favorite and is now a bit of a cult classic in the city. I'm vegan, and this is the sort of place where they're not trying to imitate meat but pay homage to their plant-based menu. I've taken all of my meat-eating friends—you know the sort who smirk when they hear you've turned vegan as if your life has just ended—and each and every single one of them swore that this was one of the best meals of their lives. The menu is extremely diverse and international, not limited to a specific cuisine. The atmosphere is really nice as well; it looks really pretty inside. I've tried everything on the menu, a few times! My favorite dish is the Malaysian curry with cashew nuts and yellow rice. To die for. I'm there at least once a week!

My secret to happiness:

"Music. Making it. Listening to it."

Kearon King

Singer

— *Born and bred in London, recommends...*

 ## Secret Spot
— *Brixton Market*

Brixton Market is this dynamic mix of cultures and flavors. It's not just a market; it's a vibrant hub where diverse communities come together. From trendy cafes to authentic international eateries, the culinary scene is unparalleled. The market's pulsating energy and eclectic atmosphere offer an immersive experience like no other. Whether you're savoring gourmet street food or browsing artisanal crafts, every visit is an adventure. It's a testament to London's cosmopolitan spirit and the epitome of urban cool. Brixton Market isn't just a destination; it's a lifestyle, embodying the essence of modern London. I visit at least once a week for a meal or to shop.

🍴 Favorite Restaurant
— *Bleecker Burger Victoria*

205 Victoria St, SW1E 5NE

Crowned with the 2024 Burger of the Year award, their signature double cheeseburger is a revelation—juicy, perfectly seasoned beef sandwiched in a pillowy bun. Pair it with their legendary house fries and creamy milkshakes for the ultimate indulgence. Conveniently located near Victoria Station.

🍷 Favorite Pub
— *The Duke of Edinburgh*

204 Ferndale Rd, SW9 8AG

This is the best pub to go to in summer because of its massive garden seating area. And if you just want to go where all the good-looking people of London flock, this is the right spot. Young, hip, and beautiful seem to coexist well there. It's a magnet for sports events, and their food is also delicious and fairly priced. But their garden is the real showstopper.

What do you like most about living in London?

❝ *I love the vibrant fusion of cultures. From the pulsing rhythms of Notting Hill Carnival to the diverse food scene in Brixton Market, every corner offers a taste of somewhere else. The energy of the city, the endless opportunities, and the sense of community make London truly special."*

Made or Born Londoner?

❝ *I was born in London and have never lived anywhere else. I've traveled a little, but there's nowhere I've been to so far that could ever compete with London."*

Secret Spot
— *Brixton Market*

My secret to happiness:

"People."

Thomas Campbell

Retired Teacher

— Born and bred in London, recommends...

Made or Born a Londoner?

❝ *I was born in Dundee, Scotland, but moved to London to study at Goldsmiths' College and just stayed on.*❞

🔒 Secret Spot
— Greenwhich Market

Greenwich Market stands out for its vibrant atmosphere and diverse offerings. Nestled in a UNESCO World Heritage Site, it boasts a rich history and an eclectic mix of stalls selling handmade crafts, antiques, fashion, art, and delicious street food from around the world. The market's unique blend of culture, creativity, and history makes it my favorite destination in London.

🍷 Favorite Pub
— Cittie of Yorke

22 High Holborn, WC1V 6BN

Near Chancery Lane tube station, this pub is a Rococo masterpiece and one of the most historic in London. It's a Grade II listed public house and is included in the National Inventory of Historic Pub Interiors. There are numerous rooms, most of which are Byzantine in style. The beer collection is sublime, and the food is outstanding. Try the fish and chips, steak and ale pie with mashed potatoes, or the onion rings.

🍴 Favorite Restaurant
— Royal Teas

76 Royal Hill, Greenwich, SE10 8RT

In Greenwich—which, as a visitor to London, you'll most likely access by boat—there's a delightful health-conscious café offering vegetarian- and vegan-friendly breakfasts and lunches, as well as tea, cakes, and freshly ground coffee. You'll have an amazing afternoon tea experience there. Everything is homemade with love, and the owners are very friendly. Greenwich is a lovely place, known as a royal borough and home to the University of Greenwich, which was formerly the Old Royal Naval College. While you're there, check out Greenwich Market, where, if you can dream it, you can buy it.

What do you like most about living in London?

❝ *London's myriad activities and diversity of people create a globally renowned heterogeneous society. Its blend of nationalities, cultures, cuisines, and lifestyles enriches life experiences. I admire and bask in its coexistence of tradition and innovation, as London cherishes its heritage while boldly embracing the future. If you're tired of London, you're tired of the world.*❞

🔒 Secret Spot
— *Primrose Hill*

From Primrose Hill, you can enjoy some of the best views of London without spending a penny. When the weather is nice, people gather on the grass, play music, and bask in the sunshine. As a Mediterranean soul, I always miss the sun in winter and soak it up in summer, and there's no place like Primrose Hill for that. It's the perfect spot to hang out with friends or for a first date.

🍷 Favorite Pub
— *The Duke of York*

2 St Ann's Terrace, NW8 6PJ

In the upscale neighborhood of St. John's Wood, this pub offers a genuine London experience. It embodies everything a good pub should be: great Sunday roasts, colorful characters, and wonderful staff. Perfect for lunch or dinner any day of the week with your mates, except during cricket season when it can get a bit crowded for my taste.

My secret to happiness:

"Live in the moment; it prevents stress from accumulating."

Ilias Marinopoulos
Dentist

— *Born in Greece and moved to London for work, recommends...*

What do you like most about living in London?

" *London remains the beating heart of Europe, even after its departure from the EU. It pulsates with energy; if you tire of life in London, you tire of living itself. It's a vibrant mosaic of cultures. Greeks like myself, along with numerous other national and ethnic groups, feel intricately woven into this bustling community.*"

Made or Born a Londoner?

" *I have been living in London for almost a decade. I'm originally from Greece and spent time studying in Scandinavia. If London weren't my base, I would be in sunny Los Angeles.*"

🍴 Favorite Restaurant
— *The Life Goddess*

29 Store St, WC1E 7QB

In central London, near Tottenham Court Road tube station, you'll find an incredible Greek restaurant. Offering divine food, wine, coffee, and pastries, it's a true gem. The staff possess a rare talent for making guests feel at home, akin to dining at their mother or grandmother's table. Sundays feature themed parties, popular in Greece. Even without reservations, they happily accommodate large parties. Favorites include the lamb with lemon risotto, a delight for the soul. The stuffed aubergines topped with a thick layer of toasted feta are next-level wonderful. If you show interest, you can also enjoy culinary history lessons on what you just ordered, enhancing the dining experience. If you love Greek food, this is a must-visit spot in London.

Favorite
Restaurant
— *Burger &*
Lobster

Made or Born a Londoner?

 I'm originally from Derry in Ireland and came to London to study accountancy. I'm still here 27 years later."

 ## Secret Spot
— *Richmond Park*

Fantastic open park in one of the greatest cities on earth. Go to the center of the park and lie back, close your eyes, and you could be in the middle of the countryside. There is a protected view from King Henry VIII's mound. There is a telescope on King Henry VIII's mound where you can look straight over London to St. Paul's Cathedral. On some days, you can even see free-roaming deer pottering about.

Favorite Pub
— *The Churchill Arms*

119 Kensington Church St, W8 7LN

Plenty of Irish memorabilia and pictures of Churchill adorn this establishment. Located in one of the most expensive parts of London, it offers local beers for sale and a restaurant at the back serving fantastic Thai food. Depending on the time of year, the outside of the bar is adorned with either flowers or Christmas trees.

Aoife Gallagher

Accountant

— Born in Ireland and seduced by London, recommends...

What do you like most about living in London?

London's allure lies in its fusion of timeless elegance and pulsating modernity. From hidden speakeasies to bustling markets, every corner unveils a new adventure. The intertwining streets echo with history, inviting exploration, while the Thames flows as the city's lifeblood, connecting its vibrant soul."

 ## Favorite Restaurant
— *Burger & Lobster*

29 Clarges St, W1J 7EF

Sometimes, when you don't want to experiment and crave something reliably delectable, Burger & Lobster fits the bill perfectly. With a few branches, my favorite for its elegance is the Mayfair one near Piccadilly Circus tube station. Great service and even better food await. Start with the lobster croquettes, simply amazing. The lobster roll and lobster Mac and cheese are outstanding. I also love the Lake District burger, always cooked to perfection. And of course, ordering a whole lobster, steamed or grilled, is the epitome of decadence. They'll even show you how to pick out the lobster meat you didn't see so not a bit goes to waste.

London Eye,
London, 7.40 pm

My secret to happiness:

"Just being."

Rebecca Fletcher

Makeup Artist

— Born and bred in London, recommends...

Made or Born Londoner?

" *I was born in Canning Town in East London, but now I live in South Quay on the Isle of Dogs.* "

🔒 Favorite Spot
— Greenwich Park

Nestled away from the city's hustle, Greenwich Park offers serene greenery and stunning views of the Thames. Its rich history, from the Royal Observatory to the Meridian Line, adds an enchanting allure. Whether I'm strolling amidst ancient trees or picnicking on its expansive lawns, the park's tranquility rejuvenates my spirit. It's a tranquil escape where time stands still amid the city's chaos.

🍷 Favorite Pub
— The Gun

27 Coldharbour, E14 9NS

This is one of the oldest pubs in East London, opposite the Millennium Dome. It's literally on the river dock, so they still have the original cannon from which they used to fire the cannonballs. It's definitely a gastropub serving up amazing food. It's perfect in the summer to eat and drink out on the terrace. If you are not into beers or lagers, their wine selection is incredible.

🍴 Favorite Restaurant
— Cicchetti Piccadilly

215 Piccadilly, St. James's, W1J 9HL

This restaurant specializes in Italian small plates, or Italian tapas, a novel concept. The presentation is quite theatrical, but even without that, the food is amazing. There is a lot of really fresh seafood, and they just keep bringing plates until you raise the white flag and can't eat anymore. I love that the mood is really relaxed, unlike most busy restaurants in London where they are always rushing you to get out so they can turn tables faster. The service is also not contrived. They take their time to get to know you if you're dining there for the first time, or treat you like an old friend if you're a regular. One of my favorite dishes there is truffle gnocchi. When I think about it I feel like I want it right now!

What do you like most about living in London?

" *London's perpetual motion captivates me. From new shows to events and eateries, there's always something fresh. Dull routines are alien here. It's a city celebrating diversity, enriching each encounter. London's rawness, unmatched elsewhere, invigorates me.* "

Favorite Restaurant
— *Cicchetti*
Piccadilly

My secret to happiness:

"To always have a positive mental attitude."

Hazel Turner

·Bed and Breakfast Owner·

— Born in Birmingham, now based in London, recommends...

Made or Born a Londoner?

❝ *I was born in Birmingham but have been living in London for the past 30 years."*

ⓘ Favorite Spot — *Chiswick House and Gardens*

This is my sanctuary in London. Tucked away in Chiswick, it's a historic villa surrounded by meticulously landscaped gardens. The grandeur of the architecture and the tranquility of the greenery provide an escape from London's madness. I love to wander the pathways and relish a quiet moment by the lake to count my blessings.

🏆 Favorite Pub — *Tabbard*

2 Bath Rd, W4 1LW

Chilled pub with sofas and tables in the heart of the trendy neighborhood of Chiswick. They serve hearty British fare plus amazing beer, wine, and cocktail selections. You're guaranteed to either meet one of the most interesting or amusing people of your life if you go there for a drink with your guard down and an openness to be surprised.

🍴 Favorite Restaurant — *La Trompette*

3-7 Devonshire Rd, W4 2EU

This high-end modern French restaurant, offering charcuterie and foie gras dishes, is set in an aesthetically beautiful space in the heart of the buzzy neighborhood of Chiswick. Every time I go there, I know I'm going to eat food unlike anything I've ever tasted or experienced before. This Michelin-starred restaurant features a fixed-price set menu. The cured seabass starter is like poetry.

What do you like most about living in London?

❝ *I love that every corner of London has its own character and story. Having lived here most of my life, I've grown to appreciate the city's ever-changing seasons. Even in the depths of winter, there's often a crisp, sunny day that cuts through the grey and lifts your spirits. It's those small, unexpected moments that make living in London feel special."*

Secret Spot
— *Hogarth's House in Chiswick*

The former residence of artist William Hogarth, it's now a museum offering a fascinating glimpse into his life and works. Stepping through its doors feels like embarking on a journey through history, where each room tells a story of Hogarth's creativity and legacy. It's my sanctuary.

Favorite Pub
— *The Roebuck*

122 Chiswick High Rd., W4 1PU

This is a lively, young, and exciting pub in Chelsea with a leafy green garden that makes it perfect for all seasons. It's what you would call a gastropub, serving hands down the best Sunday roast you can find in London. During the weekends you can drink until midnight.

> *My secret to happiness:*
>
> *"Being grateful for the simplest things I have."*

David Yates

Delicatessen Manager

— *Born and bred in London, recommends...*

Made or Born a Londoner?

> **"** *I was born in the suburb of Chiswick in London. I've never lived anywhere else and can't imagine ever leaving."*

Favorite Restaurant
— *Villa di Geggiano*

66-68 Chiswick High Rd., W4 1SY

Quaint and delightful Italian restaurant in Chiswick specializes in high-end Tuscan food paired with organic wines. It's a little pricey, so I go there on special occasions. I love that they feature local artists and have an outdoor seating area when the weather is cooperative. The steak tartare is absolutely divine, and their pastas will be the most authentic you'll have this side of Florence.

What do you like most about living in London?

> **"** *I love that wherever you live in London, barring the really touristy parts of the city, there is always that feeling of small community living. It feels like a village, rather than one of the biggest and most cosmopolitan cities in the world. And that, I believe, is its greatest charm."*

Secret Spot
— *The Tabard*
Theatre

Made or Born Londoner?

> *I moved to London forty-seven years ago. I grew up in various parts of England. If I wasn't living in London, I'd probably be trying to!"*

🔒 Secret Spot
— *The Tabard Theatre*

This is a small 96-seat theater in Chiswick, close to Turnham Green tube station. It's an intimate venue hosting a variety of performances, from plays to comedy shows, offering an antidote to London's busy West End. Tucked away from the city's bustle, it's a hidden gem for lovers of the performing arts. Whether I'm immersed in a gripping drama or laughing at a comedy, the Tabard always leaves me with cherished memories.

🍷 Favorite Pub
— *The Copper Cow*

2 Fauconberg Rd, W4 3JY

It's not a pub per se, but a local wine bar in Chiswick. With a great mix of customers, it serves amazing beer and wine. While not fitting the typical pub description, it serves the same function. Unlike many pubs, which can be intimidating for women, this place is far more relaxed. It's equally welcoming for meeting my husband after work or my girlfriends.

My secret to happiness:
"Having diverse interests to never be bored."

Jane Atkinson

Media Advisor

— *Born in England and bred in London, recommends...*

What do you like most about living in London?

> *London's fusion of culture, art, dining, and history, coupled with its iconic river and diverse architecture, creates a dynamic city. Unique black cabs and distinct neighborhoods like Brick Lane highlight its trendsetting spirit, while green spaces and river activities enhance its charm."*

🍴 Favorite Restaurant
— *Cecconi's Mayfair*

5A Burlington Gardens, W1S 3EP

If you want effortlessly chic, combining classic Italian charm with a modern London vibe, then this is the restaurant for you. Their handmade pasta is unbeatable—the lobster spaghetti is rich and indulgent, and the truffle tagliolini is pure luxury. The atmosphere strikes a perfect balance between lively and intimate, making it ideal for a special dinner or a long, leisurely lunch. The Negronis are impeccable, and the staff make you feel like a regular, even on your first visit. It's a little slice of Venice in the heart of Mayfair.

My secret to happiness:

"To be here now"

Christina Murdock

Actor

— *Born in San Francisco and adopted by London, recommends...*

🔒 Secret Spot
— *Leighton House Museum*

Once the residence of Victorian artist Frederic Leighton, this museum's exquisite art collection and architectural beauty captivate me every visit. The tranquil atmosphere and rich history transport me to another era. Anytime the craziness of London gets to my soul, I escape here to recharge. It's not on the tourist map.

🍷 Favorite Pub
— *Elgin*

255 Elgin Ave., W9 1NJ

This is my favorite watering hole—an elegant pub with exposed brick, subway tiles, and shabby chic decor. It serves delicious pub-style food with plenty of vegan and vegetarian options. The upstairs space is stunning and perfect for wedding receptions, while baked goods and breads from a local bake shop add to its charm.

Made or Born a Londoner?

" *I moved to London from San Francisco to go to drama school. I was awarded the UK Exceptional Talent visa and have been a member of the Royal Court Theatre's Writers' Group.*"

Favorite Restaurant
— *The Shed*

122 Palace Gardens Terrace, W8 4RT

This farm-to-table restaurant showcases the finest British produce and cooking. I adore its rustic ambiance with colorful fabrics and barrels, along with its tapas-like plates. The seasonal menu keeps things exciting, but their steak and fish dishes consistently delight. And don't get me started on their sinful and addictive desserts!

What do you like most about living in London?

" *I love how easy it is to get around using the underground or buses. I love how big this city is. There are so many little villages and towns all right next to each other. Every neighborhood has its own high street. There is so much to explore, it's never-ending. I am also in awe of the history. For an American, I love that where we are standing now has been around for hundreds of years.*"

Made or Born Londoner?

> *I moved to London over seventeen years ago to learn English and to study. I loved the city so much that I decided to make it my own."*

What do you like most about living in London?

> *London is many things to many people. But once you get over the innate beauty of the city, it always comes down to the people who flock to London to make it their home that ultimately give this great city its particular flavor. The variety of backgrounds, cultures, personalities, and outlooks just make London the most magical city."*

My secret to happiness:
"To always be authentic, aware and curious, but not to judge"

Georgina
Business Analyst
— Moved to London to study and work, recommends...

 Favorite Spot
— Fryent Country Park

A short walk away from Wembley Stadium, this incredible oasis in London is a public wildlife conservation area with open fields and woods, hills, a beautiful lake, many paths, and horse stables. It feels like you have been transported to a fairytale setting. Most people who live in London have never heard of it because it genuinely feels like a well-hidden secret.

 Favorite Pub
— Radio Rooftop

336-337 Strand, WC2R 1HA

This is more of a bar on the rooftop of the ME Hotel in Aldwych. The location and the view from the bar are breathtaking. Service is impeccable, and given what you are getting, the prices for cocktails are quite fair for London. But even if they weren't, the view and the vibe more than make up for it.

 Favorite Restaurant
— Inamo

11-14 Hanover Pl, WC2E 9JP

Tucked away in a small alley off Covent Garden, this Japanese-Asian fusion restaurant offers a unique experience. It's one of the most interactive dining spots, featuring high-tech tables that entertain with memory games as you wait. The food is exceptional, and the service, typical of genuine Japanese establishments, is outstanding.

My secret to happiness:

"Not to take yourself or life too seriously"

Leah

Marketing Manager

— Born in Berlin, now based in London, recommends...

Made or Born Londoner?

 I am half English, half German and have always dreamt of living in London. Eight years ago, I finally made the move from Berlin to pursue my dream."

🔒 Secret Spot
— Carter Lane

This historic street in the heart of London runs south of Ludgate Hill and the famous St. Paul's Cathedral. Steeped in London's rich history, it echoes with tales of centuries past. From its medieval origins to surviving the Great Fire, each cobblestone holds a story. The Rising Sun, a pub at 61 Carter Lane, is a heritage-listed building worth a visit for a cold pint of beer to cap your visit.

🍷 Favorite Pub
— The Castle

38 Tooting High St, SW17 0RG

They claim to be the best pub in Tooting, and they are not lying. Recently renovated with an amazing and spacious outdoor space for a pub in London, they have these makeshift beach huts adorned with fairy lights. When the sun sets, this is the place to be. The ultimate genuine local London pub experience.

🍴 Favorite Restaurant
— El Pastor

7A Stoney St, SE1 9AA

One of the few authentic Mexican restaurants in London, situated in the Borough Market area renowned for its amazing culinary scene, you can be certain that it's the real deal. The guacamole is simple yet divine, paired perfectly with thick and crispy totopos. The five salsas are a must-try, even for those not keen on spice. The El Pastor tacos, steak quesadilla, and sea bass ceviche are all top-notch choices. The staff are attentive and friendly, swiftly refilling water, condiments, and tacos. Booking in advance is recommended due to its popularity, but it's well worth the wait. Don't miss out on their house-made Mezcal for a delightful drink experience. Overall, a fantastic dining experience.

What do you like most about living in London?

The architecture, for sure. I love how much of old London still survives, unlike Berlin, most of which was bombed in the war. London's architecture, while regal and impressive, remains accessible and non-intimidating."

Favorite Restaurant
— *El Pastor*

My secret to happiness:

"Nature."

Matt

Advertising Executive

— Moved to London for work, recommends ...

Made or Born Londoner?

" *Like most people who live here, I was drawn to London twenty-two years ago for work and quickly realized this is where it's at.*"

🔒 Secret Spot — *Wapping*

These former docks are now a diverse residential neighborhood with classic riverside pubs along the Thames. Trendy bars and upscale restaurants with outdoor seating are clustered around St. Katharine Docks marina. Tobacco Dock serves as a venue for food festivals and various events. The Thames River Police Museum offers insights into the history of London's police force.

🍸 Favorite Pub — *The Holy Tavern*

55 Britton St, EC1M 5UQ

Around since 1720, legend has it that as far back as the 1200s, there was an older inn here where the Crusaders congregated for a drink before setting off to Jerusalem. In fact, the pub used to be called The Jerusalem until recently. It's an old-school London pub with all the charm and perks that come with that, including its distinctive oval-shaped beer bottles.

🍴 Favorite Restaurant

Moro

34-36 Exmouth Market, EC1R 4QE

In the heart of the charming Exmouth Market area in Islington, this Spanish, Mediterranean, and North African fusion restaurant is an institution. From the spicy lamb and quail starters to the communal vegetable mezze, each dish offers a tantalizing array of tastes. The inviting ambiance is perfect for friends, family, or a romantic date.

" *London's unparalleled cultural and artistic scene. From internationally acclaimed museums to avant-garde galleries and theaters, London pulsates with creativity. Our diverse neighborhoods cultivate innovation and experimentation, making it a mecca for those craving the cutting edge in anything.*"

What do you like most about living in London?

Made or Born Londoner?

> *I noved to London to study at the London School of Economics, but I loved the city so much I decided to call it home. When I was younger, I lived here for a few years. That's when I caught the bug."*

My secret to happiness:

"Walking in London"

Secret Spot
— *St. Paul's Cathedral Dome*

Not many people know this, but you can actually climb the 528 steps up to the dome of St. Paul's Cathedral, through the Golden Gallery. It's incredibly peaceful inside. The panoramic view of London from its most famous cathedral puts the entire city in perspective and renews your commitment to living here.

Favorite Pub
— *Bounce Farringdon*

121 Holborn, EC1N 2TD

I'm not really a pub person, but this 1950s cocktail bar and pizza restaurant near Chancery Lane tube station in central London is a swinging joint that's good for a quick meet or a longer night out, starting with drinks and ending with dinner. Oh, did I mention they have 17 ping pong tables?

Niranjana
Consultant

— *Moved to London to study, recommends...*

What do you like most about living in London?

> *The luxury of being able to walk comfortably everywhere and anywhere, while appreciating the beauty of the city along the way."*

Favorite Restaurant
— *Took Took West Hampstead*

221 W End Ln, NW6 1XJ

If you ever find yourself in the lovely neighborhood of West Hampstead in the northwest part of London, there is a very funky pan-Asian street restaurant aptly called Took Took. I am a Pad Thai addict, and I've tried the best Thai restaurants in London and beyond, but none compare to this one. The papaya salad is another favorite of mine, along with the chili paneer, prawn gyoza, and the fire-hot chili lamb. This family-run restaurant exudes warmth in its service and homeliness in its food. Wrapping it up with a sticky toffee pudding and masala chai is quite possibly the definition of bliss.

Secret Spot
— *St. James's
Park*

Made or Born Londoner?

❝ I was born and raised in Wales but moved to London about a decade ago. London has instant charm for tourists, but to acutally live here is even better.❞

What do you like most about living in London?

❝ I love that all roads lead to London. More than any other city in the world, there is a much higher chance in London of meeting like-minded people and kindred spirits, which ultimately spurs some of the most profound friendships and relationships. And it's the kind of city that ensures you are never bored or understimulated.❞

🔒 Favorite Restaurant
— *Daddy Bao*

113 Mitcham Rd, SW17 9PE

Visitors to London must venture out to many of its vibrant, non-central neighborhoods like Tooting. There, you will find my favorite restaurant, specializing in fluffy Taiwanese buns stuffed with everything your heart can desire. My favorite is the pulled pork. It's buzzy and hip but affordable. The food speaks for itself. Best Bao in London!

🍸 Favorite Pub
— *The Antelope*

76 Mitcham Rd, SW17 9NG

Also eclectic Tooting where I live, this pub serves as a social hub for the neighborhood's young residents. It has a massive screen in the back for live sports. If you're a fan of the great British Sunday Roast, this is one of the best pubs to savor it. On Friday nights, they feature live music, mostly British folk music. Needless to say, they offer a respectable selection of beer, lager, ales, and everything in between.

My secret to happiness:

"Treat positive things as gifts and the negatives as an opportunity to learn and grow."

Ollie

Accountant

— Born and bred in Wales, now based in London, recommends...

Secret Spot
— *St James's Park*

Nestled in the heart of the city, its central location near Buckingham Palace offers a serene escape from the bustling streets. The park's beauty is unparalleled, with its lush greenery, serene lake, and vibrant flower beds. Taking a leisurely stroll along the tree-lined pathways or lounging on the grassy lawns provides a peaceful respite. Watching the elegant swans glide across the water is a lovely way to reflect, while the charming pelicans add a touch of whimsy. Whether enjoying a picnic with friends or simply basking in the tranquility, St. James's Park is always captivating with its timeless allure.

Buckingham Palace,
London, 10.47 pm

My secret to happiness:

"Not waiting for happiness to drop in your lap."

Pol

Actor

— *Born in Bareclona, now based in London, recommends...*

🍴 Favorite Restaurant
— *Sushisamba*

Heron Tower, Bishopsgate, EC2N 4AY

Located on the thirty-seventh floor of a skyscraper, this is one of the rare restaurants with a view where the food is actually amazing. I usually find that restaurants with breathtaking views just use that as a gimmick and don't care about the actual dining experience. But not here. Try to time your visit with the golden hour or sunset to really make the most of the experience. I believe the first branch started in New York in the late 1990s and then made waves across the world. This is a South American take on sushi, or a fusion of Japanese, Brazilian, and Peruvian flavors. The sushi, sashimi, and tempura dishes that you know and love but elevated and bursting with flavors and colors.

🔒 Secret Spot
— *Granary Square*

In the heart of the once-dodgy King's Cross, this expansive space provides a picturesque backdrop for hanging out, eating, or just chilling. Lined with charming cafes, exciting restaurants, and quirky boutiques, it offers a diverse mix of culinary adventures and shopping experiences. The central fountains, illuminated at night, create a mesmerizing spectacle, drawing crowds to relax by the water's edge.

🍸 Favorite Pub
— *Narrowboat*

119 St Peter's St, N1 8PZ

Close to Angel tube station, this pub has a beautiful terrace that offers charming canal views. Most run-of-the-mill pubs in London have that particular smell and low lighting that can make the experience underwhelming. But this pub is the antithesis of that. The food is really delicious, the beer is cheap and varied, and you will always run into someone interesting, amusing, or at the very least, memorable.

Made or Born Londoner?

❝ *I was born in Barcelona and moved to London ten years ago for my musical theater training."*

What do you love most about London?

❝ *London is a nonstop flow of opportunities. You can always find a way to achieve what you want and pursue your dreams. That potential excites me. But if you come from a small town or city like I do, as much as I love Barcelona, the opportunities to flap your wings and fly are just fewer. This is especially true in the creative arts industries, where I work. London is one of just a handful of cities that are considered the center of gravity if you want to make it in that world. If you are talented, London will open many doors for you, regardless of who you know."*

My secret to happiness:

"Dancing, dancing, and then dancing some more."

Shaquille

Dancer

— Born in Rotterdam, now based in London, recommends...

Made or Born Londoner?

" *I was born in Rotterdam and then moved to Amsterdam. I came to London to chase my dreams, like many others.*"

Secret Spot
— The Box Soho

This club/performance theater is notoriously difficult to get into. I'm not sure how they achieve it, but it's almost as if they curate their clientele so that at any given time, everyone there is interesting, intriguing, and exciting. They consistently showcase amazing shows, which, as a performer, nourish my soul. They also have a branch in New York.

Favorite Pub
— Vagabond Shoreditch

4 Principal Pl, Worship St, EC2A 2FA

This wine bar in hipster Shoreditch is a low-key, elegant spot where you can try different wines before you commit. Their wine selection is sublime, covering major regions like Italy, France, California, Australia, and beyond. If you're feeling peckish, their menu is delightful: small plates, artisanal cheeses, sandwiches, and charcuteries.

Favorite Restaurant
— Balans Soho, No.60

60-62 Old Compton St, W1D 4UG

If you love to eat at any time of the day, this 24-hour restaurant in the heart of the entertainment district in Soho is your best friend in London. Their contemporary European menu caters to all tastes and desires. They generally stop serving alcohol after midnight. I'm definitely NOT saying if you're a regular that this rule may be loosened for you. Wink, wink! Their Balans Club sandwich is epic.

What do you like most about living in London?

" *London goes on, and it keeps going. It's the quintessentially nonstop city. It's very similar to cities like New York, but there is something about London that touches people in a starkly different way. I am not sure if it's the profound sense of history or its European DNA that just gives it an edge over other mega-cities where important things happen. I love that everyone here is chasing a dream, and that imparts a certain magic.*"

Made or Born Londoner?

> *I was born in Indonesia and relocated to London twenty years ago for university. Like many before me and many yet to come, I made the decision to stay.*"

What do you like most about living in London?

> *I love that every time I catch up with friends, I can check out a new wine bar or restaurant. You can never complain about a routine setting here, and if you wanted, you could have a coffee, a drink, or a meal in a brand new place every single day of the year.*"

Favorite Pub
— *The Bull*

13 North Hill, N6 4AB

This delightful gastropub is located in Highgate, North London, renowned for being the burial place of Karl Marx. If you're visiting London, be sure to venture out here for a slice of heaven. With its charming outdoor area, never-ending flow of quality beer, and true to its gastropub credentials, the food is nothing short of rock and roll.

Secret Spot
— *Parkland Walk*

This green corridor in North London traces the path of a former railway line from Highgate to Finsbury Park. It's a serene escape of tranquil woodland, meadows, and wildlife habitats. I love walking, jogging, and cycling there, which is a rejuvenating contrast to London's urban sprawl. It's my essential retreat for recharging and connecting with the outdoors.

My secret to happiness:

"Never being my greatest critic."

Velicia Bachtiar

Life Science Director

— *Born in Indonesia and now lives in London, recommends...*

Favorite Restaurant
— *Morito*

32 Exmouth Market, EC1R 4QE

Morito in Exmouth Market is a tapas and mezze bar influenced by Spanish and Moorish cuisine, located next to its sister restaurant Moro. With a legacy of at least twenty-five years, it remains as trendy as it is unpretentious. For aficionados of Spanish cuisine, it's unparalleled in London. The tapas selection is outstanding. Personal favorites include the fried chickpeas, beetroot hummus, anchovies with tomato salad, and spicy lamb. Don't overlook the deep-fried baby squid with sumac and alioli, and the exquisite Iberico jamon. I appreciate the thoughtful details like fresh flowers and spices on each table, coupled with heartfelt and impeccable service.

Favorite
Restaurant
— *The Golden
Hind*

Made or Born Londoner?

> *I was born in Westminster, in the heart of London, and have always called this great city home."*

 ## Secret Spot
— *Leadenhall Market*

In the heart of the City of London, this Victorian market is steeped in history and architectural splendor. Dating back to the 14th century, its ornate wrought iron and glass roof create a captivating atmosphere. Wander through its cobbled streets lined with boutique shops, charming cafes, and gourmet eateries. The market's vibrant energy and bustling ambiance evoke a bygone era, transporting you to a world of timeless elegance.

Favorite Pub
— *The French House*

49 Dean St, W1D 5BG

I frequent several, but the French House in Soho is my absolute favorite. The most offhand staff in London, and they are proud of it! The crowd ranges from retired thespians to film directors and city traders, which makes for a very cool buzz. Inside, it's a compact bar hung with photos, where the crowd prefers wine to beer and embraces a no-tech rule.

My secret to happiness:

"Family and friends."

Mark

Financial Advisor

— *Born in London, recommends...*

What do you like most about living in London?

> *London grew when a series of villages slowly melded into a city over 2,000 years. But uncannily, as you walk through London, each area still retains its unique character. I don't know of any other large city in the world where this happens."*

 ## Favorite Restaurant
— *The Golden Hind*

Cathedral St, SE1 9DE

This fish and chips restaurant in the heart of Marylebone has been around for over 100 years, and for good reason. If you're a fan of fish and chips, there's no better place in London to indulge. The portions are generous, and it's all in the way they fry the battered fish in groundnut oil—truly exemplary. While most fish and chips joints in London are tiny takeaway places, this is one of the few proper restaurants with a charming and modern interior. And if you're not into the fried stuff, there's plenty more on the menu, as well as a very exciting range of cocktails. From the side menu, the classic mushy peas are, of course, a must, but the fried feta fritters are also extremely moreish.

Cian O'Donovan

Solicitor

— Born in Cork, now based in London, recommends...

My secret to happiness:

"Enjoying the now."

What do you like most about living in London?

> *I love how you can wake up one day not knowing what to do and then, at the end of it, you find that you've done something you had never done before. London provides the opportunity to mesmerize you if only you open your eyes and let her take charge."*

Secret Spot
— *Brick Lane Food Market*

This vibrant culinary hub will set your senses ablaze with its diverse array of flavors and aromas! In the heart of East London, this market showcases the city's rich cultural tapestry through its eclectic food. From traditional, yummy curries to artisanal pastries, every corner brims with gastronomic bliss, inviting exploration and indulgence. Go hungry.

Favorite Pub
— *BrewDog*

51 Bethnal Grn Rd, E2 7GR

A short walk away from London's iconic Columbia Road Flower Market, this no-nonsense pub in trendy Shoreditch specializes in craft beers from a beloved Scottish brewery. The food consistently hits the spot, and the service is as reliable as Swiss clockwork. Additionally, they offer fantastic vegetarian options for those inclined.

Made or Born Londoner?

> *I moved to London when I was 24 years old from Cork in Ireland. Post-graduate studies brought me to London, and I never left."*

Favorite Restaurant
— *On the Bab*

305 Old St, EC1V 9LA

If you're into Korean food, there's a mighty joint in London dishing up a fusion of Korean flavors with modern twists. The ambiance is super cozy, and the service is crazy attentive. The mouthwatering Korean fried chicken and succulent BBQ meats are my drug of choice. A must-visit destination for enthusiasts of bold and innovative cuisine who don't want to mess about.

Made or Born a Londoner?

I was born in London and then moved away for many years before returning in 2015. Whether you're a native or have been adopted by the city, it leaves an indelible mark on your soul, connecting you to it forever."

🍷 Favorite Pub
— *Crown & Anchor*

22 Neal St, WC2H 9PS

Allow the inviting glow of this pub's sign to beckon you inside. It boasts a stylish ambiance and offers an extensive beer selection. Visiting during quieter hours presents the perfect opportunity to explore the world of niche breweries featured among the numerous options on tap and in bottles, or to seek recommendations from the exceptionally friendly staff.

🔒 Secret Spot
— *Ritzy Cinema*

I love to escape to the Ritzy Cinema in Brixton, which frankly is probably the best in London. It dates back to 1911 and even survived the bombings during The Blitz. And it's still standing. Besides its amazing selection of films, it's also a proud and vibrant cultural hub. With a welcoming bar downstairs, friendly staff, and the lively 'Upstairs at the Ritzy' hosting diverse events like 'Brixton Rare Soul,' you can't afford to miss this experience.

My secret to happiness:

"Embracing the art of selective amnesia!"

James

Entrepreneur

— *Born and bred in London, recommends...*

What do you like most about living in London?

From the bustling streets of Brixton, where the aromas of jerk chicken and the sounds of reggae music fill the air, to the colorful markets teeming with tropical fruits and spices, London honors my Caribbean identity and makes me truly feel at home. And it's not just Afro-Caribbeans; everyone else finds a piece of themselves here."

🍴 Favorite Restaurant
— *Turtle Bay*

382-384, Brixton Rd, SW9 7AW

Turtle Bay in Brixton is always a vibe. It's where Caribbean soul meets London energy—think reggae beats, rum cocktails, and bold flavors. Their jerk chicken is smoky perfection, and the goat curry? Rich, spicy, and unforgettable. I love their happy hour—it's dangerously good. The laid-back, vibrant atmosphere feels like a mini island escape right in the middle of Brixton's buzz. Perfect for meeting friends or just soaking up the good vibes over a Ting 'n' Sting cocktail.

My secret to happiness:
"Treat problems like piñatas - smack them and enjoy the sweet surprises that come tumbling out!"

Noura Zahrani

Life Coach

— *Born in Saudi Arabi, adopted by London recommends...*

 Favorite Restaurant
— *Club Gascon*

57 W Smithfield, EC1A 9DS

Renowned since 1998 for its exceptional duck and foie gras, Club Gascon is my favorite restaurant in London. These days, it embraces sustainability with a revamped menu, including a section featuring veg-focused dishes. Duck remains a highlight, particularly the foie gras terrine served with banyuls and fig. Other options, like roasted sturgeon and roast grouse, always hit the mark, and the kitchen excels with evil desserts. Wine pairings are sublime, and the restaurant's timeless modernity ensures longevity. If you like indulgence and forward-thinking in one place, this is your London restaurant.

Made or Born Londoner?

" I was born in Saudi Arabia and moved to London for a few months, but ended up staying. I have been here for more than thirteen years."

What do you like most about living in London?

" There are many great cities in the world. But there is something about London that touches your soul and heart at a deeper, visceral level. The city has a way of projecting its greatness without making too much of a big deal about it, which leads most people to believe they can make it here. And most do."

 **Favorite Pub**
— *The Bunch Of Grapes*

207 Brompton Rd, SW3 1LA

In the heart of the affluent neighborhood of Knightsbridge, a stone's throw away from the famous Harrods department store, is this quaint wooden-floored watering hole that has been one of the few constants in the neighborhood. They have a covered patio, floor-to-ceiling windows, and in winter, they light up their real fireplace. Not to be missed.

Secret Spot
— *Tate Modern*

This museum holds a special place in my heart. Its avant-garde exhibitions and dynamic installations offer a glimpse into the ever-evolving world of contemporary art. Its iconic industrial architecture, juxtaposed with the modern artworks within, creates a unique atmosphere that inspires and challenges me. Whether exploring the galleries or lounging by the riverside terrace, it's my sanctuary of creativity.

My secret to happiness:

"Take what the world has given me as a gift."

Peter

Financial Advisor

— *Adopted by London, recommends...*

Made or Born Londoner?

Lived in London before moving to San Francisco, and then I moved back to London after I got married."

Secret Spot — *Brown Hart Gardens*

Just off Duke Street in Mayfair is a 10,000 square foot public garden situated atop an electricity substation. Where else in the world would you find such a unique setup? I visit for a peaceful picnic or a relaxing lunch break. There's ample seating and a distinctive raised layout that provides a serene ambiance.

Favorite Pub — *Blue Posts*

6 Bennet St, SW1A 1RE

This classic neighborhood London pub near Green Park is tucked away from the hustle, despite being in Central London. For anyone visiting London, this is the perfect antidote to the tacky tourist-trap pubs that lack soul or character. Their service is top-notch, and their selection of beers, wines, and, of course, food is as good as it gets. Despite the location, prices are fair, making it ideal for repeat visits.

Favorite Restaurant — *Casse-Croûte*

109 Bermondsey St, SE1 3XB

This quaint eatery near London Bridge is a rustic French experience with a cozy atmosphere. Their daily menu of French classics offers three options per course at reasonable prices. I love the salmon rillettes and herbed lamb. Cheese and charcuterie plates available for lighter appetites. Expect to leave smiling and fully satisfied. Ah, quel délice!

What do you like most about living in London?

You can stroll down any street, in any neighborhood, and spend an entire day immersed in a medley of languages other than English. While many perceive London as the quintessential symbol of Britain, it's, in fact, a symbol of the world."

Favorite Pub
— *The Anglesea Arms*

15 Selwood Terrace, SW7 3QG

An incredible local gastropub and alehouse in South Kensington, beloved by residents. I highly recommend booking in advance as it's always packed. The menu is sublime and seasonal. The duck terrine starter is particularly tasty, and their Sunday roast is delightful. I have a weakness for their sticky date pudding, perhaps a bit too much!

Secret Spot
— *Hampstead Obervatory*

This is my haven amidst the city chaos, where I escape into the vastness of the universe. Gazing at stars and planets grounds me in awe and wonder amidst the urban jungle. It's best to check the observatory's schedule in advance as it may vary depending on weather conditions and special events.

Made or Born Londoner?

I was born in Moscow but moved to London thirteen years ago to work for a bespoke auction house. Moscow and London are the two great loves of my life!

What do you like most about living in London?

London's allure lies in its perpetual reinvention. It's a living canvas where every corner whispers a new story. From the ever-evolving skyline to the buzzing energy of its streets, there's an undeniable sense of opportunity and excitement. In London, the present is always pregnant with possibility.

My secret to happiness: *"Finding joy in the unexpected"*

Victoria

Auctioneer

— *Born in Moscow, now lives in London, recommends...*

 ## Favorite Restaurant
— *The Delaunay*

55 Aldwych, WC2B 4BB

A sophisticated dining experience awaits with a timeless European-inspired menu. Whenever I crave a classic schnitzel or decadent pastries, I head there. Perfectly situated for pre-theater dining in the heart of the West End, its elegant ambiance and attentive service make it ideal for intimate dinners or celebratory gatherings. Whether it's breakfast, brunch, lunch, or dinner, it's a great choice!

Favorite
Restaurant
—*Claude Bosi at
Bibendum*

Made or Born Londoner?

> *I was born in London and never left. Witnessing the city's evolution intertwined with its unflinching traditions has been breathtaking.*"

> *I cherish the city for its ceaseless evolution, akin to a living organism. Every corner teems with innovation, art, and new experiences. It's a perpetual playground where old meets new, tradition intertwines with modernity, and creativity knows no bounds. London's dynamic energy fuels my spirit, offering endless opportunities for exploration and growth, ensuring that boredom is an impossibility in this vibrant metropolis.*"

What do you like most about living in London?

My secret to happiness: *"Bottomless gratitude for what I have."*

Robert

Chef

— Born and bred in London, recommends...

 Favorite Restaurant — *Claude Bosi at Bibendum*

81 Fulham Rd., SW3 6RD

A French restaurant where you're treated like royalty. The modern décor and Michelin-inspired French posters set the scene. Seafood by Michelin-star Chef Claude Bosi is outstanding. The seabass is the juiciest ever, and foie gras creatively paired with egg yolk is magical. Friendly staff cater to your every need, and the sommeliers are spot-on. Not cheap, but worth every penny. A special occasion sort of place. Sometimes in life, you need to treat yourself.

 Secret Spot — *Bishops Park*

This picturesque riverside oasis along the Thames in Fulham is my haven. With charming walkways and a serene atmosphere, it's been around since 1893. I adore its riverside strolls, picnic opportunities on the grassy lawns, and leisurely boat rides. Despite its historic significance and scenic beauty, it remains an oasis of peace.

 Favorite Pub — *The World's End*

174 Camden High St, NW1 0NS

I don't drink anymore, but if I did, this would be my pub of choice. Situated in Camden Market, the world's largest pub doesn't disappoint. It offers a great atmosphere, music, and beer. The staff are friendly, and the cozy interior with cool decor makes it perfect for winter. Live music enthusiasts will adore it.

St. Paul's Cathederal,
Rome, 6.50 p,

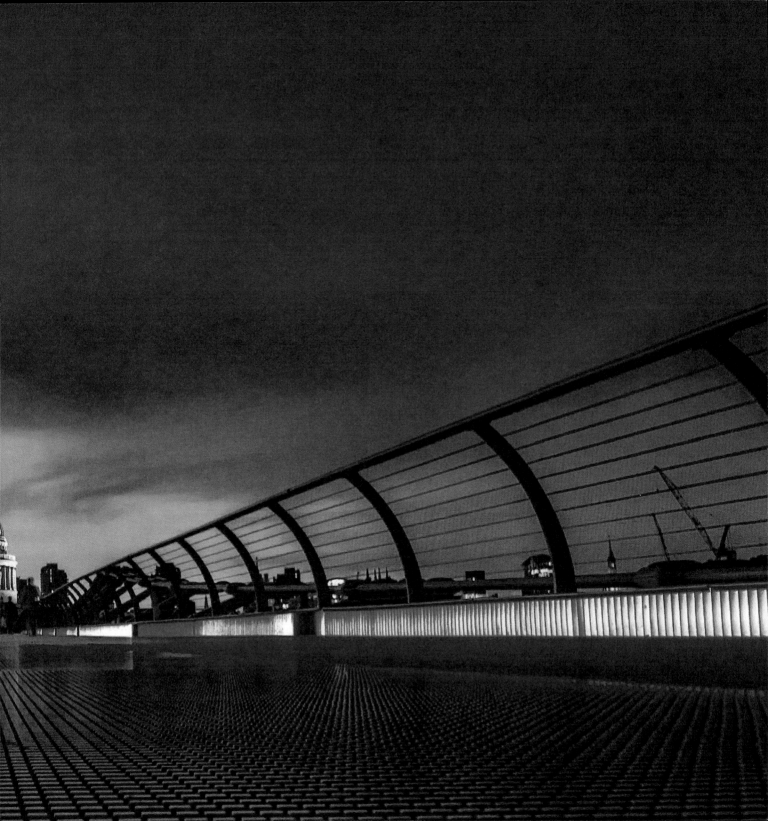

My secret to happiness:

"To appreciate what life has generously given me without taking it for granted."

Pipa Hawthorne

Marketing Manager

— *Born in Surrey and lives in London, recommends...*

🔒 Secret Spot
— *Fulham Palace*

This historic palace in West London offers a captivating blend of history, architecture, and natural beauty. Once home to bishops, I adore its stunning gardens, museum, and archaeological remains. While guided tours and exhibitions are available, I prefer getting lost in its picturesque gardens. It's also the perfect place to spend a magical day with loved ones or family.

🍷 Favorite Pub
— *The Dickens Inn*

Marble Quay, St Katharine's Way, E1W 1UH

An amazing gastropub in the heart of St. Katherine's Dock. Smart menu choices, fair prices, and a stellar collection of beers, wines, and spirits are the main attractions here. Even without reservations, they always strive to provide the best seats with the finest views. The incredible waitstaff and refined clientele elevate this pub experience to a higher level.

Made or Born Londoner?

> *I was born in Surrey and moved to London when I was eighteen. I've lived briefly in Milan and Berlin before making my way back to London."*

What do you like most about living in London?

> *Its eccentricity keeps me hooked; from quirky street art to impromptu performances, there's always something delightfully unexpected lurking around the corner. A truly thrilling city that gives more than it takes."*

🍴 Favorite Restaurant
— *Ishbilia*

8-9 William St, SW1X 9HL

If, like me, you crave Lebanese food and obsess over hummus, this joint in Belgravia will hit the spot. Apart from the hummus, I dream of their chicken shish tawook and courgettes with yogurt, along with starters like Beirut-style hummus, falafel, and grilled halloumi. Knafe for dessert was a standout—I never share it!

My secret to happiness:

"To accept that pain and sadness are also part of life."

Hugh F. Anderson

Writer

— Born in Cambridge, based in London, recommends...

Made or Born Londoner?

> *I was born in Cambridge and moved to London ten years ago. London is a hub for media, and it's also a rite of passage for many people to move here after university."*

🔒 Secret Spot — *Kyoto Garden*

A serene Japanese garden nestled inside Holland Park, gifted from Kyoto, Japan, in 1991. I escape there to be healed by its tranquil ponds, lush greenery, and traditional architecture. Complete with a waterfall, traditional lanterns, and even peacocks and cranes, it's a haven. In Autumn, the Japanese maple trees look truly magnificent.

🍷 Favorite Pub — *The Havelock Tavern*

57 Masbro Rd, W14 0LS

This pub in the South Kensington area is your quintessential speakeasy, a relaxed social hub to wind down. I've learned that Londoners are, for the most part, monogamous with their pubs. Once they find one they love, it's a marriage for life. Inside, it's spacious, with a pretty garden and a fireplace to warm both body and soul. Amazing Sunday roasts as well.

🍴 Favorite Restaurant — *Chutney Mary*

73 St James's St, SW1A 1PH

The best meal I've had in London, if not ever, was at this Indian restaurant in the St. James neighborhood. I wasn't previously a fan of Indian cuisine, but this restaurant converted me into a believer. It's also vegetarian heaven, with generous portions, superb vibes, and friendly staff. Plus, it's fine dining that won't break the bank.

What do you like most about living in London?

> *I'm enamored by the city's endless opportunities for literary pursuits. From renowned publishing houses to vibrant literary festivals, London offers a fertile ground for honing my craft and networking with fellow wordsmiths. Every street corner is a potential source of storytelling magic.*

Made or Born Londoner?

" I was born in East London, in Whitechapel, and lived there until I was five. Then, my family moved to Archway in North London. I've been living in this city for all of my fifty-two years. "

My secret to happiness:
"Understanding that there aren't any universal truths."

🔒 Secret Spot
— *Canary Wharf*

This major financial hub epitomizes modernity and ambition. Skyscrapers pierce the skyline, symbolizing economic prowess and innovation. Yet, it's not just for suits; you'll find diverse dining, shopping, and cultural experiences. From artisanal coffee shops to world-class restaurants, there's something for everyone. I love photography, and its dramatic skyline always inspires me. It's like a mini Manhattan in London.

🏆 Favorite Pub
— *Spread Eagle*

141 Albert St, NW1 7NB

In the center of Camden town, this classic Victorian-style pub has a varied array of beers, ciders, ales, and wines, accompanied by a delectable gastro menu. The ambiance is buzzy, setting the perfect mood for the weekend. The staff are consistently friendly. Whether it's a laid-back evening or an animated night out, this pub reliably provides an outstanding experience.

Leon

University Administrator

— Born and bred in London, recommends...

What do you like most about living in London?

" I am very passionate about photography and urban design. I love living in London for its eclectic architecture, vibrant street life, and constant evolution. Every corner tells a story, offering endless inspiration for capturing the essence of urban living and design diversity, making every day a new adventure. "

Favorite Restaurant
— *Ibérica Marylebone*

195 Great Portland St, W1W 5PS

The trend-setting tapas restaurant is under the guidance of Executive Chef Nacho Manzano, renowned for his numerous Michelin stars. He brings his signature dishes while introducing fresh selections. Among my favorites are the paella Valenciana, patatas bravas, trío de jamón ibérico, and, of course, churros with chocolate. The spring onion tempura, served with lemon aïoli and soy, is exceptionally delicious. Beer, cider, sangria, and an extensive variety of sherries and cava by the glass seal the deal.

Favorite
Restaurant
—*Dishoom*

🔒 Secret Spot
— *AIRE Ancient Baths London*

Inspired by the bathing traditions of ancient Roman, Greek, and Ottoman civilizations, this hidden oasis in central London is where I love to escape when I feel the need to reward myself or get a lift-me-up. I adore the tranquil ambiance, featuring thermal baths, steam rooms, and massage therapies. Every aspect, from the hypnotic music to the attention to detail, combines to offer a blissful escape.

🍷 Favorite Pub
— *Sir Richard Steele*

97 Haverstock Hill, NW3 4RL

Just north of central London, this Haverstock Hill pub is extremely dog-friendly. It has a laid-back atmosphere, with no television screens, so it doesn't cater to the rowdy sports crowd—if that's not your thing. It isn't mine. The food is consistently excellent and fairly priced. As an American, it's hard for me to admit that you can have the best burger at an English pub. Often, they have incredible, rockin' live music.

My secret to happiness:

"Keep your smile well-oiled with laughter and your heart seasoned with gratitude."

Made or Born Londoner?

> *I am originally from Chicago but moved here for work. It took a bit of adjustment, but London is home now."*

Shane

Business Consultant

— Born in the USA, now lives in London, recommends...

What do you like most about living in London?

> *Compared to Chicago, I love London's seamless blend of old-world charm with modern vibrancy. Public transportation works and makes exploring* effortless. *The architectural juxtaposition, from historic landmarks to contemporary structures, as well as the bustling markets and diverse culinary scene, continually surprise and delight me."*

🍴 Favorite Restaurant
— *Dishoom King's Cross*

5 Stable St, N1C 4AB

This chain of upscale Indian restaurants totally redrew the Indian food scene in London when they launched their first spot in Covent Garden in 2010. I prefer their King's Cross branch in Granary Square because it fits perfectly with the incredible urban redevelopment of that part of town, which, many years ago, used to be rather seedy. Unless you're a hermit living under a rock, you've heard of Dishoom. If you're only having one meal in London, have it there, even if Indian food is not your thing. Trust me, the black dahl is pure culinary magic.

My secret to happiness:

"Staying busy, family joy, quiet village life, tiny peaceful garden."

Jean Broke-Smith

Etiquette Teacher

— Born in Sussex and bred in London, recommends...

Made or Born Londoner?

"Born in Sussex, I ventured to London at seventeen, joining Lucy Clayton's to pursue modeling. Later, studying art and fashion kept me in the city, where I've resided for over forty years."

🔒 Secret Spot
— *Brick Lane Street*

This bustling street in London's East End is a captivating fusion of cultures and artistic expression. Here, you'll find a diverse array of curry houses, vintage shops, and vibrant street art. It's a magnet for food enthusiasts, artists, and fashion lovers alike, offering a dynamic blend of tradition and innovation that embodies the spirit of London.

🍷 Favorite Pub
— *The Castle*

100 Holland Park Avenue, W11 4UA

This pub serves exceptional home-cooked food. I'm a frequent visitor, relishing their delicious offerings for lunch. Their efficiency and quality are impressive, making it a favorite spot in Notting Hill, which itself is well worth a visit. I'm particularly discerning about sandwiches, and theirs never disappoint—they're a testament to their commitment to excellence.

🍴 Favorite Restaurant
— *Lucio Restaurant*

257-259 Fulham Rd., SW3 6HY

This Italian restaurant on Fulham Road in Fulham offers exceptional cuisine. It's renowned for its connection to San Lorenzo, frequented by celebrities like Jack Nicholson and the late Princess Diana. The menu is flexible, the wine list superb, and the staff excellent. It maintains high standards, reflecting Lucio's previous managerial role. Whether it's on the menu or not, they cater to your preferences. Run by a family, it exudes warmth and hospitality. Over the years, it has become my favorite spot for Italian food, offering not just a meal but an experience where you might even spot a celebrity dining alongside you.

What do you like most about living in London?

In our international city, people stand out for their friendliness. Lost? Someone will assist. There's a genuine goodness. Walking takes time because of the familiar faces; there's a strong sense of community and camaraderie."

Made or Born a Londoner?

> *I was born in Chiswick, which is the posh part of Hammersmith— we like to think!"*

🔒 Secret Spot
— *Ronnie Scott's Jazz Club*

Established in 1959 by saxophonist Ronnie Scott, the iconic Soho venue is a cornerstone of London's music scene. Scott, a pioneering figure in British jazz, created the club as a platform for emerging and established artists alike. The atmosphere is vibrant, and the performances are world-class. After six decades, it remains a beloved London institution.

🍷 Favorite Pub
— *The Mitre*

40 Holland Park Ave, W11 3QY

A Holland Park institution, combining a relaxed, welcoming atmosphere with a touch of elegance. Their selection of craft beers and wines is excellent, and the food is spot-on—try the fish and chips or the roasted chicken for a comforting classic done perfectly. The cozy interior makes it a great spot for a catch-up, but if the sun's out, their outdoor seating is ideal for people-watching on the avenue.

> My secret to happiness:
> *"Always anticipating new projects, embracing what brings joy, and seeking adventure and love."*

Christopher Stock
Musician

— Born and bred in London, recommends...

What do you like most about living in London?

> *London's dynamic vibe evolves with time. It's the convenience of proximity to beloved amenities, though often underutilized, like museums. I cherish the music scene, especially jazz and blues. Living here is an exhilarating experience."*

🍴 Favorite Restaurant
— *Pizza Express Jazz Club*

10 Dean St, W1D 3RW

The inaugural restaurant of this beloved chain in Soho boasts an iconic jazz club in the basement. Witness great American, European, and British jazz artists performing in a casual atmosphere. While the food is consistently good, the primary draw is unquestionably the music.

My secret to happiness:

"Not to take anything for granted and to keep the kid inside of me always alive."

Alison Adkins

Nurse

— Born in Essex and based in London, recommends...

Made or Born Londoner?

> *I was born in Essex and moved to London when I was ten with my family. I've been a proud Londoner ever since and have not looked back."*

🔒 Secret Spot
— *Dublin Castle*

Established in the 1970s, this iconic Camden music venue shaped British indie music, hosting Oasis, Amy Winehouse, and Coldplay. Rumored to have launched Madness, it offers cheap drinks before 6 p.m. Each visit is unique; I savored cold beer while listening to 70s rock. This is also one of the best places to discover new British music right before it explodes into the limelight.

🍷 Favorite Pub
— *The Coach & Horses, Soho*

29 Greek St, W1D 5DH

If I had to pick one pub in London to hang out in forever, this is it. It's been around since the 19th century and has a cool, bohemian vibe. The sort of place where Dylan Thomas and George Orwell used to knock back pints. They've always got a bunch of different beers on tap, and the conversations here are always buzzing with life.

🍴 Favorite Restaurant
— *Zeret Kitchen*

216-218 Camberwell Rd, SE5 0ED

Looking for culinary adventures? This South London gem in Camberwell offers authentic Ethiopian cuisine in a lively setting. From savory stews to tasty flatbreads, every dish bursts with flavor. The staff warmly guide you through the menu. And don't worry about etiquette – it's all about digging in with your hands! Generous portions and reasonable prices make it a must-visit. Whether you're an Ethiopian food lover or newbie, gather your pals and dive in!

What do you like most about living in London?

> *As a mother of two toddlers, I adore the city's endless opportunities for enriching experiences. From world-class museums to vibrant parks, there's always something to be amazed by. The diverse community fosters acceptance and understanding, providing my children with a multicultural upbringing, which, in the world we live in, is needed more than ever."*

My secret to happiness:

"Good coffee, amazing wine, and a strong woman to love."

Tunde Adeyemi
Medical Student

— *Born in Nigeria, now based in London, recommends...*

Favorite Restaurant
— *Kudu*

119 Queen's Rd, SE15 2EZ

One thing you grow to love about London is the mind-boggling variety of ethnic cuisines. And African food is alive and well in this great city. My favorite restaurant in London, where I always seem to have the best meals of my life, is a South African tapas-like place in Peckham, which, as a neighborhood itself, seems to be the gravitational center of great African food. Kudu also happens to be an extremely elegant and well-thought-out eatery. Just because it's a neighborhood place, it doesn't mean it's homely. Start with their signature bread and the different types of butter. Don't miss out on the onglet steak, and their cured trout is also a slam dunk.

Made or Born Londoner?

I was born in Nigeria, and moved to London when I was five."

Secret Spot
— *Peckham Rye Park & Common*

This Victorian gem in South London has formal gardens, woodlands, and a serene lake. Lots of family-oriented amenities and a dog-friendly policy. An indoor and outdoor café serves amazing meals. Charming flower gardens and peaceful canals make it a haven for nature lovers like me.

Favorite Pub
— *Prince of Peckham Pub*

1 Clayton Rd, SE15 5JA

Also in Peckham is this amazing Caribbean fusion pub. This is not the sort of boozer where you go to relax or have a quiet drink. It's well and truly alive, and if you are in the mood to mingle, dance, or meet new and exciting faces, this is the pub for you. The food is amazing and will exceed your expectations of pub food.

What do you like most about living in London?

I cherish the vibrant tapestry of African culture that envelops me daily in this great city. From the rich aromas of Nigerian cuisine to the rhythmic beats of Afrobeat echoing through the streets, I feel connected to my roots. It's a comforting embrace, making this bustling metropolis feel like home."

Made or Born Londoner?

" *I was born in London. My family moved to Malaysia for the first eighteen years of my life. I came back to study.*"

What do you like most about living in London?

" *I relish its vibrant energy. Exploring eco-friendly cafes, cycling through the city's green spaces, and advocating for sustainable practices give me purpose. Amidst the hustle, I find solace in contributing to a greener, more sustainable future for our planet. London has a long way to go, but at least I am here, being part of the change.*"

🔒 Secret Spot
— *Viktor Wynd Museum of Curiosities*

This Hackney museum is a quirky treasure trove. It's like stepping into the mind of an eccentric collector—filled with everything from taxidermy to oddball art pieces. It's not your usual museum, and that's exactly why I love it. The cocktail bar upstairs is a fun bonus, making it the perfect mix of weird and wonderful for an afternoon escape.

🍸 Favorite Pub
— *Viajante87*

87 Notting Hill Gate, W11 3JZ

In Notting Hill', this bar celebrates sustainability in every aspect. From eco-friendly cocktails to recycled glass furnishings and upcycled cork walls, it prioritizes green initiatives. Its experiential cocktail menu revolves around a zero-waste ethos, focusing on innovative agave-based drinks. A must-visit for those seeking a sustainable London cocktail experience.

My secret to happiness:

"Giving more to the planet than taking."

Natasha McGill

Science Student

— *Born and bred in London, recommends...*

🍴 Favorite Restaurant
— *Tofu Vegan Islington*

105 Upper St, N1 1QN

This down-to-earth vegan restaurant, situated in Islington in the northern part of central London, recreates classic Chinese favorites using solely plant-based ingredients. I was never a fan of mock-meat until someone introduced me to this incredible place. Meat-lovers and committed carnivores swear by it. It wouldn't be hyperbole on my part to describe it as one of the best restaurants in London. You have to trust me and try it. They have exceeded expectations for a vegan restaurant. The wontons with their house sauce will warm your heart.

Favorite
Restaurant
— *The Ivy*

Made or Born Londoner?

> *I was born in Devon and moved to London when I was a teenager for my father's job.*

🔒 Secret Spot
— *Kenwood House*

Originally constructed in the 17th century, Kenwood House in Highgate boasts a rich history spanning centuries. The estate features stunning neoclassical architecture and a remarkable art collection, including works by Rembrandt and Vermeer. I admire its picturesque grounds, curated gardens, and captivating interiors. While you're there, make sure to visit the famous Highgate Cemetery, a short walk away, where Marx was buried.

🍷 Favorite Pub
— *The Audley*

41-43 Mount St, W1K 2RX

If you enjoy your drink served with gorgeous art, this pub in Mayfair is perfect for you. Divided into three art-centric spaces—a ground-level pub, a restaurant above, and upper floors for private gatherings—the theme here is a rotating display of significant artworks. The food is terrific, so a solid choice for a Sunday roast or lazy weekday lunches and early dinners.

Terry Somerville

Surgeon

— *Born in Devon, now based in London, recommends...*

What do you like most about living in London?

> *The city's diverse art and cultural offerings feed my soul. From the quaint galleries of Mayfair to the experimental showcases in Shoreditch,* London's artistic tapestry never fails to enthrall. The city's rich history intertwined with its contemporary performances in West End theaters is the icing on the cake. Access to art is London's magical allure.*

🍴 Favorite Restaurant
— *The Ivy*

1-5 West St, WC2H 9NQ

This long-standing restaurant in Covent Garden is as iconic as London itself. Founded in 1917 as a pre-theater destination, it quickly became a favorite hangout for celebrities. This is still very much the case, so be wary if you are easily star-struck. But its glamorous history and reputation aside, this remains a great British establishment, shaming anyone who dares ridicule British food. If you must dine somewhere elegant in London, make it The Ivy. I love the cottage pie and chicken breast with truffle filling. Their desserts are all devilish, and the espresso martini is a must. Breakfast, lunch, and dinner are dynamite.

Notting Hill Carnival

My secret to happiness:

"Knowing that I am the master of my fate and that change is inevitable."

Andy Coghill

Neuroscientist

— Born and bred in London, recommends...

What do you like most about living in London?

" That if you can dream of it, you can probably achieve it or find it in this city. There is a reason why London is the European center of excellence for many things."

Secret Spot
— Horniman Museum

Nestled within the lush surroundings of Forest Hill lies this lesser-known treasure in London's museum landscape. Delve into its diverse collections showcasing artifacts from across the world. Additionally, you can enjoy attractions such as an aquarium, a butterfly house, and frequent complimentary activities, particularly during school breaks.

Favorite Pub
— The Lighthouse

441 Battersea Park Rd, SW11 4LR

This airy pub in Battersea features original art, gastropub food, and a leafy garden. You can even bring your dog! I had the very best spicy margarita there. The food is excellent, especially the Tarka Dahl. There's a new roof terrace, attentive staff, and a welcoming vibe. Highly recommended for a true London vibe.

 ### Favorite Restaurant
— A Toca

341 Wandsworth Rd, SW8 2JH

A few years ago, an ex-girlfriend from Portugal introduced me to her country's cuisine at A Toca in Stockwell, also known as Little Portugal. This is a delightful celebration of no-nonsense, authentic Portuguese fare like grilled pork belly, smoked sausage, and the classic bacalhau a bras.

Made or Born Londoner?

" I was born in North London, and with the exception of a few years studying in the United States, I have always lived here and suspect I will continue doing so."

Secret Spot—
Horniman Museum

My secret to happiness:

"Food made from the heart and shared with those I love."

Riddhi

Personal Chef

— *Born and bred in London, recommends…*

Made or Born Londoner?

Secret Spot
— *Battersea Power Station*

An amazing transformation of an urban eyesore, blending history with modern flair. The iconic architecture echoes its gritty past. Now bustling with shops, eateries, and entertainment. The food court is outstanding, and the cinema rivals London's best. Don't miss this must-visit spot, offering a unique blend of past and present delights.

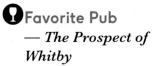

Favorite Pub
— *The Prospect of Whitby*

57 Wapping Wall, E1W 3SH

This is potentially the oldest pub along the River Thames, tracing its roots to circa AD 1520 in Wapping. Rebuilt since, remnants of its original flagstone floor endure. Once dubbed "the Devil's Tavern" for its dubious clientele and activities like cockfighting, it's now a charming riverside establishment with maritime-inspired decor.

Favorite Restaurant
— *Amaya*

19 Motcomb Street, SW1X 8JT

One of London's four Michelin-starred Indian spots, this Belgravia gem defies expectations with its bang-for-buck offerings. They want to make Indian food the go-to for wallet-friendly dining. Meticulously crafted dishes, served platter-style for lunch and dinner, hit the spot perfectly. And trust me, their black pepper chicken tikka is downright addictive. Drooling right now.

What do you like most about living in London?

I am in awe of its refusal to settle for mediocrity. The city's relentless pursuit of excellence means you're always surrounded by the best—whether it's food, culture, or innovation. From world-class dining to cutting-edge entertainment, London offers nothing but the finest experiences, making everyday life truly extraordinary."

Made or Born Londoner?

> *I was born in Geneva to Egyptian diplomatic parents. I moved to London to study, and like many of my compatriots, I fell in love with the city and chose to remain."*

My secret to happiness:

"When I allow myself to be a little girl again."

Secret Spot
— *Petrie Museum of Egyptian Archaeology*

A treasure trove of Egyptian artefacts. Literally, thousands. Okay, it's not as slick as the British Museum, but because it's part of the University College London campus, it's totally free. Its collection includes everyday objects like jewelry and pottery, as well as a remarkable array of funerary artifacts such as sarcophagi and shabtis.

Favorite Pub
— *The Barley Mow*

82 Duke St, W1K 6JG

In the heart of Mayfair, this 19th-century heritage listed pub was recently refurbished while maintaining its vintage pub ambiance. The food is excellent and affordable, with a plentiful and varied selection of drinks. Upstairs, a restaurant offers British classics like steamed cockles and daily roasts, providing a convenient dining option for a complete night out.

Amal Wahba

Economist

— *Originally from Egypt, now based in London, recommends...*

What do you like most about living in London?

> *At one point, the British Empire aspired to dominate the world. When that endeavor concluded, an unexpected result was that the world converged on London, rather than vice versa. The fact that you don't have to be English to feel completely at home in London is what I love most about this city."*

Favorite Restaurant
— *Koshari Street*

56 St Martin's Ln, WC2N 4EA

Long before vegetarianism or veganism became trendy, Egyptians embraced plant-based diets for ages. The humble Egyptian dish, Koshari, symbolizes this tradition. Legend suggests Egypt's Jewish community created it as kosher-friendly street food. Living in London, I craved this hearty mix of rice, lentils, pasta, chickpeas, topped with tangy tomato sauce, and crispy fried onions. Koshari Street in Covent Garden recreates Cairo's magic—it's pure delight.

Loving London
— *Pub life*

Made or Born Londoner?

❝ *I was born in Edinbrugh to a Swedish father and a Scottish mother. I moved here fifteen years ago.*❞

What do you like most about living in London?

❝ *Its abundance of green spaces offers a breath of fresh air amid the urban hustle. From Hyde Park's serene lakes to Hampstead Heath's panoramic views, the city provides tranquil escapes and easy access to nature for rejuvenation and relaxation. Compare this to a city like New York, where their only green outlet is Central Park.*❞

ⓘ Secret Spot
— *The Top Secret Comedy Club*

Deep in the heart of London's West End theater hub, this no-frills comedy club isn't just my secret spot; it's my secret to happiness. Laughing is a balm for the soul. I've seen celebrity performers and stand-up comics debut here, going on to make a name for themselves. Treat yourself and catch a show there.

🍷 Favorite Pub
— *The Cow*

89 Westbourne Park Rd, W2 5QH

The Cow is a classic gastropub with a relaxed yet stylish vibe. Known for its seafood, their dressed crab and Guinness are a winning combo. The interiors have that charming, slightly lived-in feel, and the crowd is always lively but never overwhelming. It's the kind of place where you can grab a drink at the bar or settle in for a long, indulgent meal. Quintessential West London.

My secret to happiness:

"Carbohydrates. Especially when delivered through wine."

Freja Lindström
Physiotherapist

— *Born in Edinbrugh, now based in London, recommends...*

🍴 Favorite Restaurant
— *Beit el Zaytoun*

Via Alberto Cadlolo, 101

This could be London's finest Lebanese restaurant, offering cold and hot mezze dishes alongside their set menus. I often visit for breakfast, choosing the fried eggs, balila, fava beans, cheeses, and jams. Their falafel, babaganoush, hummus, and chicken shawarma set the gold standard.

My secret to happiness:

"To wind down in special places with the people dearest to me."

Imogen

Photographer

— Born in Dorset, lives in London, recommends...

 Favorite Restaurant
— *Fogo de Chão Soho*

34-36 King Street, WC2E 8JS

Fogo de Chão Soho is a meat lover's paradise. The Brazilian churrasco-style dining experience is unmatched—succulent cuts of beef, lamb, and chicken carved tableside until you say stop. The salad bar is packed with fresh, vibrant options, but the real star is the picanha, cooked to perfection every time. The atmosphere is lively, the service warm and attentive, and the caipirinhas are the perfect pairing. It's the kind of place that turns dinner into an event.

Made or Born Londoner?

❝ *I was born in Lyme Regis, Dorset, renowned for its fossil-rich cliffs, charming harbor, and scenic coastal walks. However, I eventually moved to London to follow my heart and never left."*

What do you like most about living in London?

❝ *London always feels like the early stages of a steamy, passionate love affair, and it never gets old. For a big, vibrant city, it has a gentle, caressing quality that's hard to explain. Some big cities sap your energy and demand constant vigilance. London, on the other hand, feels like it's always rooting for you. Like it always has your back."*

ⓘ Secret Spot
— *National Theatre*

It's always delightful to attend a performance here. Located on the South Bank of the Thames, whatever performance you catch here will never leave you disappointed. It's excellent value compared to the exuberant prices of London's West End venues. Last show I saw was *Underdog: The Other Other Brontë*, an irreverent retelling of the life and legend of the Brontë sisters.

♀ Favorite Pub
— *The Devonshire*

17 Denman St, W1D 7HW

This Soho gastropub is steeped in history since 1793. Downstairs, the vibe is cozy, with bacon sandwiches and house-made sausage paired with expertly poured pints of Guinness. Upstairs, the grill restaurant boasts a lively atmosphere, centered around a wood ember grill, offering revamped pub classics and perfectly aged steaks.

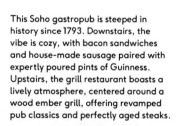

Made or Born Londoner?

> *I was born in West Kensington, London. I've traveled extensively for work but have never once entertained, let alone acted upon, the idea of leaving this vibrant city.*

🔓 Secret Spot
— *Hampton Court Palace*

This majestic royal residence in Richmond is rich in history spanning over 500 years. It was King Henry VIII's magnificent palace and is now open to the public. The stunning architecture, lush gardens, historical exhibitions, and immersive experiences offer a glimpse into England's royal past.

🍷 Favorite Pub
— *Forza Wine*

133A Rye Ln, SE15 4BQ

This budget-friendly, elevated wine bar in Peckham distinguishes itself from typical sky bars with superior food and drinks. A stylish rooftop venue offering cocktails capped at £10 is truly remarkable. While their menu may be limited, fewer options equate to exceptional quality. I relish grazing on their delightful small plates while enjoying London's stunning cityscape views.

My secret to happiness:

"Music. And some more music."

Trevor

Sound Engineer

— *Born and bred in London, recommends...*

What do you like most about living in London?

> *I love the diversity of experiences London offers. In the morning, I might sip coffee in a trendy Shoreditch cafe; by afternoon, I could be enjoying dim sum in Chinatown. Come evening, it's Jolof rice in Peckham, and in the wee hours, a kebab and hookah around Edgware Road.*

🍴 Favorite Restaurant
— *Satay House Malaysian Restaurant*

13 Sale Pl, W2 1PX

While Malaysian cuisine might not enjoy the same popularity as Japanese, Thai, Chinese, or Vietnamese, one taste will have you hooked for life. Since 1973, this family-run Malaysian restaurant has been a staple in London, serving up all the classics alongside some hidden gems. Don't limit yourself to just satay, beef rendang, and laksa; try the daging denden—a spicy stir-fried beef and lemongrass dish with delightful caramelized flavors. And you don't need to decipher Mee Goreng, Roti Canai, or Sagu Gula Melaka; simply trust me and order them. You can thank me later.

My secret to happiness:

"Hearing and telling stories that can change your life for the better."

Hanz

Film Editor

— Born in Berlin, based in London, recommends...

Favorite Restaurant
— Veeraswamy

Victory House, 99 Regent St., W1B 4RS

You can't visit London without dining at a fine Indian restaurant. And if you're going to try one, why not visit the oldest in London, which also boasts a Michelin star and offers great value for money. I adore Veeraswamy's weekend lunch deals, which, unlike typical lunch menus, offer a wide selection of dishes to choose from. Each dish showcases impressive culinary skill and incorporates the finest British ingredients. The gilafi sheek kebab, tandoori green prawns, and angara chicken tikka are absolutely mouthwatering.

Made or Born Londoner?

" *I was born and bred in Berlin but was seduced by London twelve years ago. I moved here with no plans and just ended up never leaving.*"

What do you like most about living in London?

" *Working in the film industry, I admire how London's creative arts have transformed into a hub of excellence independent of Hollywood validation. Whether you're an artist or a storyteller, London embraces you and provides ample opportunities to thrive, regardless of your connections or surname.*"

Favorite Pub
— The Blackfriar

174 Queen Victoria St, EC4V 4EG

Near Blackfriars Bridge on Queen Victoria Street is London's most stunning pub. Dating to 1875, it nearly faced demolition in the 1960s but was saved at the last minute. Adorned with mosaics and a haunting black friar, its breathtaking interior, especially the barrel-vaulted area, is a must-see. It's like no other pub in London. As you sit to enjoy your drink, look up at the ornate ceiling and thank me.

Secret Spot
— Electric Cinema

Nestled in Notting Hill, this chic cinema epitomizes stylish viewing in London, a welcome departure from ordinary multiplexes. Established in 1910, it features luxurious leather armchairs, footrests, and a bar offering cocktails, wine, and snacks. A must-visit for film buffs craving a slice of cinema history, showcasing both blockbusters and indie films.

My secret to happiness:

"Love, good food, family and travel."

Alex Bishop

Banker

— Born and riased in London, recommends...

Made or Born Londoner?

" *I was born in Chiswick, where I spent most of my life. Now, I live in Highgate in North London."*

Favorite Pub
— *The Prince Alfred*

5A Formosa St, W9 1EE

In Maida Vale since 1856, this pub is minutes from Little Venice's canals and Warwick Avenue Station. It's evident why this stunning pub is heritage-listed and protected. With a beautifully lit dining room centered on an open kitchen, the food surpasses typical pub fare. The basement's original coal cellars starred in many music videos you may have seen.

Secret Spot
— *Greenwhich Foot Tunnel*

This underground passageway beneath the River Thames in London connects Greenwich and the Isle of Dogs. Built in 1902, it offers pedestrians a unique and historic way to cross the river. You will surely love this engineering marvel, appreciate its historical significance, and enjoy stunning river views during your visit to Greenwich.

Favorite Restaurant
— *Sông Quê Café*

134 Kingsland Rd, E2 8DY

If you are a pho-head like me, this Vietnamese place on Kingsland Road has a hip, vibrant ambiance and clientele ranging from families to locals. Authentic flavors, impeccable textures, and top-notch quality make it one of the best Vietnamese joints in London.

What do you like most about living in London?

" *London is the queen city of visceral experiences. I have traveled to the far corners of the earth, but my most memorable moments, cherished experiences, and satisfying achievements occurred here. This is where I have fallen hopelessly and madly in love with the woman of my life."*

🍴 Favorite Restaurant
— *Lemonia*

89 Regent's Park Rd, NW1 8UY

This iconic Greek restaurant near Primrose Hill is everything you would want in your friendly local Greek eatery. Bright like the sun does double duty there, even during the cloudiest days. I love the grilled halloumi, spanakopita, and charcoal-grilled meats. They use high-quality Greek produce. Their star dish is the humble vegetable moussaka, embodying the restaurant's essence: rustic yet virtuous.

🔒 Secret Spot
— *St Martin-in-the-Fields Church*

Located in Trafalgar Square's north-east corner, this stunning church, designed by James Gibbs, boasts Neoclassical, Palladian, and Corinthian styles with Greek-inspired columns and an impressive façade. Its vaulted crypt hosts a popular café and music events, supporting programs for the homeless.

💡 Favorite Pub
— *The Albert*

11 Princess Rd, NW1 8JR,

Minutes from Primrose Hill, offering the best views of London, this pub is a hidden gem with a gorgeous garden area. Built around 1850, it has been renovated to showcase its Victorian DNA. The food is delicious, and I often bring my granddaughters here after a trip to the London Zoo, which is just around the corner. Fish and chips galore!

My secret to happiness:

"A good book and a dead phone."

Helen Warren
Retired

— Born and bred in London, recommends...

Made or Born Londoner?

❝ *I was born in Finchley in London. When I was younger, I spent some time in Africa, but London is home.*"

What do you like most about living in London?

❝ *I love that I can't answer this question and be 100 percent honest. That's the sort of city London is; it gives you myriad reasons to love her, and each one is equally as important. Are there things I don't like? Sure. But they pale in comparison.*"

Favorite
Restaurant
— *Galvin La*
Chapelle

Made or Born Londoner?

❝ *I was born in Manchester and moved to Cambridge for university, and eventually to London for work twenty years ago.*❞

What do you like most about living in London?

❝ *What truly stirs my soul about this city is its timeless grandeur and rich tapestry of history. From the cobblestone streets to the towering spires, London's essence is steeped in the whispers of the past. Every nook and cranny tells a story, making each stroll through its streets a journey through time.*❞

🔒 Secret Spot
— *Imperial War Museum*

War is not fun, but this museum is totally worth a visit. It offers a compelling journey through the tumultuous history of warfare. Through immersive exhibits, artifacts, and personal stories, you gain profound insights into the impact of conflict on individuals and societies. Beats the bloody wax museum!

🍷 Favorite Pub
— *The Parakeet*

256 Kentish Town Rd, NW5 2AA

In North London near Kentish Town, this is a culinary-led pub and dining room with a cozy vibe. Expect modern European dishes cooked over fire on their custom grill, like spider crab croquette and wood-roasted rabbit with kohlrabi and curry leaf. Housed in the former Victorian landmark pub, The Oxford Tavern, it maintains its local charm. It's always a treat, and you will love it too.

My secret to happiness:

"Expensive whiskey. Especially when it's gifted to me!"

Harry Pembroke

Entrepreneur

— *Born in Manchester, now based in London, recommends...*

🍴 Favorite Restaurant
— *Galvin La Chapelle*

35 Spital Square, E1 6DY

This may be London's most affordable Michelin-starred restaurant. Nestled amidst the sleek towers of the financial district, this charming red-brick ex-school offers timeless French classics amidst Victorian charm. This is a special occasion sort of joint. The best way to eat there is to trust the chefs and follow their lead. The starter of Gnocchi is impeccable. The Beef Fillet Rossini, flawlessly cooked, was elevated by the oyster emulsion, while the gratin could bring tears to your eyes.

London is renowned for its unique music scenes. Grime, a blend of electronic music and rap from East London, gained momentum with artists like Dizzee Rascal and Stormzy. Garage, with its rhythmic beats, has influenced artists like Disclosure and Jessie Ware.

My secret to happiness:

"Live in the moment. Try to relish doing less sometimes!"

Milly Kenny-Ryder

Writer, Photographer, Food Stylist

— Born and bred in London, recommends...

 ### Favorite Restaurant
— Hélène Darroze at The Connaught

Carlos Pl, W1K 2AL

Hélène Darroze is a French chef with no fewer than six Michelin stars to her name, three of which are at this restaurant, located in an elegant hotel in the heart of Mayfair. She has two stars at Marsan par Hélène Darroze in Paris and one at Hélène Darroze à Villa La Coste in Provence. I usually only eat roast at home, typically made by my dad, but I absolutely love her Sunday roast chicken menu. It was nothing short of exceptional—traditional but with a twist. Needless to say, reservations are a must, well in advance. Remember, this is not a food pit-stop but a culinary experience.

Made or Born Londoner?

❝ *Born in London and grew up here; I've always lived here. London is home."*

What do you like most about living in London?

❝ *Its charm lies in its rich diversity, offering a wealth of experiences, many of which are free. From prestigious museums and gourmet dining to cozy cafes and vibrant exhibitions, the city beckons with endless opportunities for exploration."*

Favorite Pub
— The Pelican

45 All Saints Rd, W11 1HE

I'm not a big drinker, but my family is from Provence, so probably a glass of rosé. I love hanging out at this pub in Notting Hill. It's been around since 1870 and recently underwent a makeover. The vibe is laid-back with comfy seats and vintage decor. Chef Owen Kenworthy musters delicious modern British dishes like spit-roast celeriac and monkfish pie with lobster head gravy.

Secret Spot
— Seven Dials

I enjoy wandering alone through these seven atmospheric cobbled streets in Covent Garden. First stop: Choosing Keeping for stationery, then Arome for pastries, and Monmouth for coffee. Neal's Yard holds nostalgic memories from my childhood, shopping on weekends, and singing at nearby opera houses.

Secret Restaurant
— *Hélène Darroze at
The Connaught*

My secret to happiness:
"Savoring life's simple pleasures, like sharing food with loved ones."

Aysha

Film Student

— *Born in Lisbon and based in London, recommends...*

Made or Born Londoner?

" *I was in born Lisbon, then moved to Toronto for my father's job. We relocated to London when I was seven. I still have ties to Canada, but London is home."*

🔒 Secret Spot
— *BFI Mediateque*

This gem in London invites you to dive into the enchanting realm of film and TV for free. Located in a discreet part of the British Film Institute, it allows you to immerse yourself in nearly 100,000 titles from their prestigious National Archive. It's open to everyone, whether you're studying, researching, or simply seeking free entertainment!

🍷 Favorite Pub
— *Ye Olde Cheshire Cheese*

145 Fleet St, EC4A 2BP

This 16th-century pub in the heart of London is irresistibly charming. Its low ceilings and dark wood paneling transport me to another era. What I love most is its literary ambiance, enriched by past literary giants. The hearty fare and cozy atmosphere keep me coming back. As a visitor, this may be the only pub you need to visit.

🍴 Favorite Restaurant
— *BRAT Restaurant*

4 Redchurch St, E1 6JL

This Basque-themed restaurant in Shoreditch offers a casual fine dining experience centered around a charming open wood fire grill. Famous for their turbot, and their burnt cheesecake is a dream come true. Booking in advance is recommended, as walk-ins are nearly impossible.

What do you like most about living in London?

" *The city's vibrancy makes it easy to forge lasting connections. From cozy pubs to bustling markets, there's always a chance encounter waiting to blossom into a friendship. London's diversity ensures my social circle is as rich and varied as the city itself."*

Secret Spot
— *Mudchute Park and Farm*

Located in London's Isle of Dogs, this oasis offers a serene escape from urban life. With a diverse array of animals, interactive experiences, and sprawling green spaces, it's ideal for solo visits or family outings. Nature enthusiasts seeking rural tranquility in the heart of the city will find it here. Remember to respect the animals, as this is where they live, not a zoo!

Favorite Restaurant
— *Berenjak Soho*

27 Romilly St, W1D 5AL

Compact and casual, this Persian restaurant is one of the best in London. their amazing value feasting menu includes a baklava ice cream sandwich that will spoil you for any other dessert. Their grilled meats, their safron rice, and their housemade breads are everything you drool about when you think of Persian food.

My secret to happiness:

"My secret stash of Nutella."

Elisa

Art Director

— *Born and bred in London, recommends...*

Favorite Pub
— *Ye Olde Mitre*

1 Ely Ct, Ely Pl, EC1N 6SJ

Tucked away in Holborn, this is London's most hidden pub. Built in 1546 as a tavern for the servants and retainers of the Palace of the Bishops of Ely, it has retained much of its traditional charm. I love enjoying a cold beer in their delightful courtyard on sunny days. Amazing range of ales and great food are, of course, a given.

Made or Born Londoner?

" *I was born in London to a Canadian mother and Lebanese father. I am fully English as well as a proud Lebanese-Canadian. London is the sort of city that allows for that fusion of identity.*"

What do you like most about living in London?

" *The Victorian architecture envelops London streets with its ornate facades, intricate details, and towering spires. It evokes a sense of awe and nostalgia, connecting me to a bygone era of elegance and grandeur, weaving a tapestry of history and beauty through our streets. It's the one thing I miss when I travel.*"

Favorite
Restaurant
— *Kiln*

Made or Born Londoner?

❝ Born and raised in London. I have moved away a few times for studying or work but London always draws me back.❞

 Favorite Pub
— *The Duke's Head*

8 Lower Richmond Road, SW15 1ER

A beautiful Victorian pub with original features including etched glass partitions and wooden alcoves, overlooking the river at Putney. A great selection of beers and classic British dishes on the menu, and a relaxed crowd. There is a terrace on the river for warmer evenings and a log fire indoors for cozy winter drinking.

🔒 **Secret Spot**
— *Barbican Conservatory*

A lush oasis in the midst of the Brutalist architecture of the Barbican Centre. There are around 1,500 species of plants and trees from around the world, as well as fish and terrapins in its three pools. The juxtaposition of the concrete building and the tropical foliage and beautiful flowers is really striking and sets the Barbican Conservatory apart from more traditional botanical gardens.

My secret to happiness:

"Good food, good friends and the odd chocolate bar."

Sheba Rosier

Civil Servant

— Born in London, recommends...

What do you like most about living in London?

❝ It's a cliché but I love the diversity and openness of London. I have chosen to bring up my two daughters in this city because I want them to live amongst people from all walks of life and from all four corners of the world, and to know that this city accepts everyone. For me, being a Londoner is a state of mind.❞

 Favorite Restaurant
— *Kiln*

58 Brewer Street, W1F 9TL

A fantastic restaurant in Soho offering no-fuss northern Thai cuisine with influences from Myanmar, Laos and Yunnan. The ingredients are impeccably sourced from the UK, including British grown Thai and Chinese vegetables and herbs. The best place to sit is the counter where you can watch the drama of the food being cooked in the wood-fired kiln and clay pots. The food is served in small plates so you can sample a range but don't miss the clay pot baked glass noodles with pork and crab, or smoked mackerel and lemongrass salad. No reservations but it's worth queuing up for.

My secret to happiness:

"Living in London."

Percy

Taxi Driver

— Born and based in London, recommends...

Made or Born Londoner?

"I doubt you'll find anyone more Cockney than me. Born and raised right here in London."

🔒 Secret Spot — *Spitalfields Market*

This East London market is a must-visit. It's a fantastic blend of history and modern flair, with beautiful Victorian architecture and a lively vibe. You'll find everything from vintage fashion and unique crafts to incredible street food from around the world. It's one of those spots where there's always something interesting to see and experience.

🍷 Favorite Pub — *Chesham Arms*

15 Mehetabel Road, E9 6DU

In the heart of Hackney, this cozy, character-filled pub with a welcoming atmosphere is my happy place. Enjoy real ales, local beers, and a charming beer garden. Though there's no kitchen, you can order pizza for delivery with the amazing Yard Sale Pizza. Rescued by the community from closure, it's a spot with deep local roots and plenty of authentic charm.

🍴 Favorite Restaurant — *The Quality Chop House*

92-94 Farringdon Rd, EC1R 3EA

This historic spot has been around for 155 years, serving up classic British dishes in a beautifully preserved Victorian setting. Known for its daily-changing, seasonal menu—think tender rib-eye and flavorful roasts—it's ideal for a memorable meal. With its vintage interiors and hearty flavors, this is British dining at its finest.

What do you like most about living in London?

Living in London is like breathing air—you don't always notice it, but it's essential to who you are. London is the pulse that shapes how I see the world. Sure, people grumble about the grind of city life, but how many could genuinely imagine, let alone act on, leaving it behind? It's part of who we are."

Made or Born Londoner?

> *I was born Chester near the Welsh border and moved to London as a toddler.*

What do you like most about living in London?

> *London brings out the best version of you through its layers and hidden corners. The city's energy pushes you to adapt, be curious, and embrace your individuality. It's a place that encourages quiet ambition, where each neighborhood feels like a new chapter and every encounter a chance to discover yourself profoundly.*

🔒 Secret Spot
— *Bang Bang Oriental Foodhall*

On Edgware Road is London's largest Asian food court, and it's a must for food addicts like me. With over 25 vendors serving up everything from Chinese dim sum to Japanese ramen and Korean BBQ, there's so much to explore. The lively space seats 450, making it perfect for gathering and sampling authentic flavors from across Asia. Top tip is to not gorge on one thing so you can try it all!

🍺 Favorite Pub
— *The Camden Head*

2 Camden Walk, N1 8DY

Hands-down my favorite pub in London, in Islington. Founded in 1849, it's in a charming Victorian heritage-listed building. They serve seriuus pub classics: proper fish and chips, sausage and mash, and even a great veggie burger. They've got comedy nights upstairs, so you get deadpan British humor with your pint. It's perfect!

My secret to happiness:

"Friday night."

Oliver Hastings

Engineer

— *Born in Chester, now lives in London, recommends...*

🍴 Favorite Restaurant
—*Fallow*

52 Haymarket, SW1Y 4RP

Located in London's St. James's Market, Fallow has been a culinary highlight since its opening in 2020. Founded by chefs Jack Croft and Will Murray, both alumni of Dinner by Heston Blumenthal, the restaurant emphasizes sustainability and innovative cooking. Their menu features dishes like the signature cod's head with sriracha butter, reflecting a commitment to nose-to-tail dining. The sleek, modern setting complements the creative cuisine, making it perfect for a memorable meal. I love their breakfasts, which I think is one of the best in the city.

My secret to happiness:

"Stay open and kind. Appreciate the little things."

Michela Barbieri

∞∞ Mathematics PhD student ∞∞

— Born in Italy, based in London, recommends...

Made or Born Londoner?

I am Italian but grew up in Germany. I moved to London to be a student. I wouldn't live in any other city."

 Secret Spot
— *Kenwood Ladies' Bathing Pond*

On a lovely summer day, I love nothing more than setting up a picnic blanket in one of the many meadows there and immersing myself in nature. I love the public swimming ponds, especially the chill atmosphere at Kenwood's Ladies ponds. There are women of all ages there, as well as ducks. It's not a glamorous activity, and that's part of what I love about it!

Favorite Pub
—*The Mayflower*

117 Rotherhithe St, SE16 4NF

My local pub holds a special place in my heart! Overlooking the Thames, English pilgrims departed from here on the Mayflower, bound for America in 1620. It exudes character with art, photographs, and knick-knacks. The staff are quintessentially English, witty, and friendly. Enjoy candlelit romantic dinners alongside exquisite British food, including their amazing Sunday Roast.

Favorite Restaurant
— *Takagiya*

102 Fortune Green Rd, NW6 1DS

If I could afford it, I'd be there every week! This small independent place, run by a married couple from Japan, serves authentic and outrageously delicious Japanese food. Nowhere else compares. Yuko the wife is incredibly sweet and essentially runs the place. Makoto the husband is the sole chef. You can't go wrong with anything on the menu, but my favorite things to order are the warm eggplant with saiko and hachou miso sauce, and the seared yellowtail tataki with ponzu and chopped shiso.

What do you like most about living in London?

I love how big my world is here. On a random weekend you can get so far and explore vastly different and beautiful places in under an hour. From theatre to ballet to food to gigs to random art workshops. London is a great place to be to find yourself and to be able to be who you really are, especially when you are a young adult."

My secret to happiness:

"Avocado toast."

Betina

Environmental Researcher

— Born in Frankfurt, raised in Rome, and now based in London, recommends...

🍴 Favorite Restaurant
— *The Ivy Café in Marylebone*

96 Marylebone Ln, W1U 2QA

The Ivy has a touch of classic British charm, drawing on its rich history since 1917. Originally famed for its West End location, The Ivy represents London's sophisticated dining. Marylebone's café brings that legacy to a relaxed, neighborhood setting, just a short walk from Daunt Books, which is my secret spot in London. They offering quality food and attentive service. I go for their British-inspired favorites like the crispy duck salad, shepherd's pie, and their signature chocolate bombe in a warm, timeless atmosphere.

Made or Born Londoner?

" *I was born in Frankfurt to Swiss-Italian immigrant parents, then moved to Rome, and eventually London to study. I knew from the first year that this was the city I was meant to live in."*

🔒 Secret Spot
— *Daunt Books Marylebone*

I'm a bit of a geek, so this iconic bookstore is my special haven. It feels like a different era, with beautiful interiors featuring oak balconies and skylights that cast a warm glow over rows of carefully curated books. Everything is organized by country, creating a literary journey around the world. It's cozy, unique, and the perfect place to lose yourself.

📍 Favorite Pub
— *The Marquis*

51-52 Chandos Pl, WC2N 4HS

A small, wedged pub that was rebuilt in 1843 in the heart of the city. It's a family-owned independent pub with all the charm that comes with it. Word is that Charles Dickens used to wind down here. But what is not a rumor—and certainly happened—is that a few years ago, the American band Green Day just showed up and performed. Don't miss this.

What do you like most about living in London?

" *I love the abundance of green spaces and the easy access to the countryside. You can lose yourself in vast parks like Hampstead Heath, feeling miles away from the city. And just a short train ride away, you find places like the Cotswolds—a stunning escape with rolling hills, charming cottages, and scenic walking trails. It's the perfect blend of nature and city."*

🔒 Secret Spot
— *National Portrait Gallery*

Nothing is more "London" than seeing the faces of its most iconic figures, from queens to rock stars, all under one roof. The collection is amazing, and there's always something new with the rotating exhibits. Plus, the location near Trafalgar Square is perfect for a day out in London.

🔑 Favorite Pub
— *Betjeman Arms at St Pancras*
Euston Rd., N1C 4QL

A classic British pub with charm and history. Named after the poet John Betjeman, it offers a cozy atmosphere and a great selection of ales. The menu features hearty British dishes like fish and chips and delicious pies. Set in the stunning St. Pancras station, it's the perfect spot to enjoy a meal and soak in the literary connection.

Made or Born Londoner?

❝ *My parents met in Athens and immigrated to Manchester, where they had us. My dad's job took him to London, where we've been since I was a few years old.*❞

What do you like most about living in London?

❝ *London sometimes feels like a movie set, surrounded by iconic landmarks and familiar scenes. Places like Tower Bridge, Notting Hill, or Piccadilly Circus, feel like I'm part of a story unfolding. There's a magic in recognizing these spots.*❞

My secret to happiness:

"Remaining tolerant and accepting of others."

Andrew Katsaros

Currency Trader

— *Born in Manchester, now based in London, recommends...*

🍴 Favorite Restaurant
— *Opso*
10 Paddington St, London W1U

There are plenty of Greek restaurants in London, but this one in Marylebone seduces your taste buds with its daring, modern take on Greek cuisine. The dishes are made for sharing with indulgences like crispy feta tempura with zesty lemon marmalade and loukoumades drizzled in sweet, sticky lavender honey. The lively atmosphere and open kitchen set the scene for an unforgettable experience. Every bite feels a little forbidden. It's a stylish, sensual spot for authentic Greek flavors—perfect for sparking some chemistry on a date or turning up the heat with friends. Reservations are a must.

Favorite
Restaurant
— *Dim Sum Duck*

Made or Born Londoner?

 I was born in Hong Kong and came to London as a post graduate student. I was able to find a job that made me stay.

Secret Spot
— *Museum of Brands*

I'm fascinated by the history of pop culture, and the Museum of Brands is my go-to place to journey through decades of packaging, advertising, and iconic products, seeing how brands evolved from Victorian times to today. It's a nostalgic trip through time, perfect for history buffs, designers, and anyone interested in the impact of branding on our lives. One visit isn't enough—you'll love spotting products from "your decade".

Favorite Pub
— *The Duck and Rice*

90 Berwick Street, Soho, W1F 0QB

What's more London than a unique blend of English pub vibes and Chinese cuisine? Located in Soho, the Duck and Rice is a warm, cozy traditional pub that just happens to serve an authentic Chinese menu. The Guardian praised their "game-changing dumplings," and I couldn't agree more. Perfect for a casual night out with a twist.

My secret to happiness:

"Books, films, good wine, and lifelong friends."

Peter Cheung

Business Consultant

— *Born in Hong Kong, now based in London, recommends...*

What do you like most about living in London?

London has endless things to offer, from its vibrant arts scene and fascinating history to its diverse neighborhoods and green spaces. It's a city that invites you to explore at your own pace, constantly uncovering something new. Whether it's a hidden café or a historic site, the more you experience London, the deeper your connection grows.

Favorite Restaurant
— *Dim Sum Duck*

124 King's Cross Rd, WC1X 9DS

Believe the hype—this Cantonese spot in King's Cross is worth the wait! Inside, it's a lively scene with Londoners in the know. Go for the juicy prawn dumplings, massive xiaolongbao, and classics like roast duck and beef ho fun. The portions are generous, and every bite bursts with authentic flavor. And don't skip the razor clams with garlic and vermicelli in an amazing umami broth! Prices are reasonable too, making it a fantastic spot for indulging without breaking the bank.

London is one of the greenest cities of its size in the world, with 47 per cent of the city consisting of green spaces. This includes parks, gardens, nature reserves, and other open areas, which span over 35,000 acres in total. Some of the largest and most famous green spaces include Hyde Park, Regent's Park, Richmond Park, and Hampstead Heath.

My secret to happiness:
"Gelato."

Angela

Writer

— Born in Edinbrugh, now lives in London, recommends...

Made or Born Londoner?

" *I am originally from Edinburgh. I moved to London for my postgraduate studies. I kept moving back and forth until love made me pick one!"*

🔒 Secret Spot — *Camden Passage, Islington*

If you are after a charming, vintage experience away from the crowds, this quaint pedestrian lane is lined with antique shops, cozy cafes, and unique boutiques. It's ideal for leisurely browsing, finding rare collectibles, or enjoying a coffee. I love its old-world charm and seek refuge there as a break from London's bustling heart.

🍸 Favorite Pub — *The Nag's Head*

10 James St, WC2E 8BT

This pub is a Covent Garden classic. It's got this wonderfully unpretentious vibe—small, cozy, and perfect for escaping the crowds after a day exploring the area. The staff are friendly, the beer is cold, and the atmosphere feels like a proper old-fashioned London pub. I always grab a pint of ale and people-watch from the snug by the window. It's a little slice of tradition.

🍴 Favorite Restaurant — *Brasserie Zédel*

20 Sherwood St, W1F 7ED

Zédel is a stunning art deco gem, perfect in a charming 1930s building. Enjoy the lively atmosphere with live jazz, a classic French 75, and delicious French dishes like snails in garlic butter. Start with a cocktail at Bar Américain, then dive into the prix-fixe menu—a fantastic deal for a classic Soho experience.

What do you like most about living in London?

" *The surprising warmth of its people. Despite the London's vastness and pace, I've found genuine connections everywhere—from chats with strangers in cozy pubs to friendships forged through shared interests. Moving from Edinburgh, I feared loneliness, but London's openness and its vibrant, diverse community have made it feel like home from day one."*

62

My secret to happiness:

"To try something new at least once a week."

Francis Alpert

Retired Physician

— Born and based in London, recommends...

Made or Born Londoner?

> *Born and raised in London, I dreamed in my youth of moving somewhere far, like Australia or America. It only took a little growing up to realize I was already in the best place in the world."*

🔒 Secret Spot
— *Little Venice*

Little Venice is the perfect respite from the madness of London. It's essentially a charming canal area near Paddington lined with colorful narrowboats, cozy cafes, and waterside pubs. Take a stroll along the picturesque waterways or hop on a boat to Camden. Oozong with charm and tranquility. Keep an eye out for the resident swans and canal wildlife

🏆 Favorite Pub
— *The Harwood Arms*

Walham Grove, SW6 1QJ

In the heart of Fulham, this spot is a paradise for food lovers. It's London's only Michelin-starred pub, offering a relaxed, welcoming vibe and refined, seasonal British dishes. Think fallow deer with celeriac and juniper, or a richly spiced venison Scotch egg. Pair it with English sparkling wine or a classic British ale for the full experience.

🍴 Favorite Restaurant
— *Darcie & May Green*

Grand Union Canal, W2 6DS

While you're at Little Venice, I recommend dining at this canal-side gem that brings Australian flair to London. Known for its lively brunch scene (including a famous bottomless brunch), it's perfect for a weekend visit. Try the Fancy Bacon Roll or Coconut French Toast. For a more relaxed vibe, go early in the morning or on weekday afternoons. I sometimes stop by for a laid-back evening drink too; they have a lovely selection of colorful cocktails.

What do you like most about living in London?

> *I adore London for its timeless charm—it's a city that never loses its allure. No matter how often I leave, there's never a moment when I feel drawn away for too long. I might enjoy other incredible cities when I travel, but they only make me appreciate London's beauty even more, always pulling me back home."*

🔒 Secret Spot
— *God's Own Junkyard*

Hidden in Walthamstow, this quirky gallery glows with vibrant, vintage neon signs, art pieces, and playful displays by the late artist Chris Bracey. It's perfect for exploring or snapping unforgettable photos, with a cozy café on-site. For a colorful escape from the city's usual sights, it's a must-visit!

♀ Favorite Pub
— *The Royal Vauxhall Tavern (RVT)*

372 Kennington Ln, SE11 5HY

An iconic LGBTQ+ venue in London with an electric atmosphere. Their drag shows, cabaret, and live performances are legendary. With its historic charm and unforgettable entertainment, RVT offers a warm, inclusive space that's as vibrant as it is welcoming. They have a great selection of drinks, including well-crafted cocktails, beers, and spirits.

My secret to happiness:

"To always spread love, not hate."

Kenny

Tour Guide

— *Born in Leeds, living in London, recommends…*

Made or Born Londoner?

❝ *I was born in Leeds and moved here for love. I tried convincing my partner to move to Leeds, but London was more convincing!"*

What do you like most about living in London?

❝ *I love London's endless layers. Each neighborhood, each street holds its own history, quirks, and energy. No matter how long I live here, there's always something new to uncover—a hidden garden, a cozy pub, a bustling market. The city constantly surprises me, making every day feel like an adventure."*

🍴 Favorite Restaurant
— *Samad Al Iraqi Restaurant*

284-286 Kensington High St, W14 8NZ,

If Lebanese food is all you know of Middle Eastern cuisine, you're missing out on one of the region's most irresistible delights: Iraqi food. Tucked away in a charming part of London, this spot teases and pleases with every bite. Start with complimentary lentil soup and warm, soft bread before sinking into the Kubbah Halab—crispy rice balls stuffed with spiced minced lamb and a whisper of cardamom that'll leave you craving more. The lamb kebabs and masgouf (grilled fish) are juicy, satisfying, and full of flavor. And if, like me, you live for happy endings, the baklava or kunafeh will finish you off beautifully.

Favorite Restaurant
— *Iran Restaurant*

Made or Born Londoner?

> *I was born in France. I came to London on a holiday when I was little and fell in love with it. Years later, I now call it home.*

What do you like most about living in London?

> *London's food scene. From bustling markets with flavors from every corner of the world to elegant restaurants redefining British cuisine, there's always something to satisfy any craving. Whether I'm in the mood for a classic Sunday roast or experimental street food, London never disappoints—it's a true playground for food lovers.*

🔒 Secret Spot
— *Petersham Meadows*

Nestled beside the Thames in Richmond, this serene escape from the city's bustle is famous for its grazing cattle and stunning riverside views. The meadows offer a timeless, picturesque setting perfect for a leisurely walk or picnic. Just steps from Petersham Nurseries and Richmond Hill, it's a peaceful spot that feels like you've switched off the big, crazy city!

🍷 Favorite Pub
— *Roebuck*

130 Richmond Hill, TW10 6RN

Roebuck in Richmond is a pub like no other, offering one of the most stunning views in London. Perched atop Richmond Hill, it overlooks the lush Thames Valley, a scene that's breathtaking year-round. Pair the scenery with a cold pint or a hearty Sunday roast, and you've got the perfect spot for relaxation and beauty.

My secret to happiness:

"My children."

Alice Madere

Chesmistry Teacher

— *Born in Montpellier, now based in London, recommends...*

🍴 Favorite Restaurant
— *Iran Restaurant*

25-27-29, Shepherd Market, W1J 7PR

If you're craving the best Persian food in London, this spot in Shepherd Market is a must-visit. Nestled in Mayfair's charming, historic enclave, it offers incredible dishes like perfectly cooked lamb chops (a standout favorite!), tender kebabs, and freshly baked Taftoon bread. Generous portions include flavorful starters like Mirza Ghasemi and Shirazi Salad. Finish with authentic Persian ice cream and Faloudeh. Friendly service and nostalgic vibes complete the experience!

My secret to happiness:

"Traveling somewhere new that takes my breath away."

Fiona Jamesen

Marketing Specialist

— Born in Leicester, now lives in London...

Made or Born Londoner?

I was born in Leicester and moved to London to study and work. I think you'd struggle to find someone who wasn't born elsewhere but now proudly calls this fine city home!"

🔒 Secret Spot
— *Painshill Park*

Less than an hour from London, this stunning 18th-century landscape garden is filled with surprises. The highlight? The magical Crystal Grotto, a sparkling wonder of glittering crystals and shimmering reflections. Perfect for a serene escape, you can wander through picturesque grounds, admire the Gothic tower, and soak in the beauty of this peaceful retreat.

🍷 Favorite Pub
— *The Colonel Fawcett*

1 Randolph S NW1 0SS

This place is tucked away from the busier streets of Camden, with a fantastic beer garden that's perfect for the summer. Their gin selection is impressive, and they make a mean Sunday roast. It's got that laid-back charm that makes you want to stay for one more drink... and then maybe another. I totally have not hooked up with any good-looking guys there. Ever!

🍴 Favorite Restaurant
— *Gauthier Soho*

21 Romilly St, W1D 5AF

Gauthier Soho is a masterpiece of vegan fine dining, helmed by Alexis Gauthier, a chef who truly lives his plant-based ethos. The elegant townhouse setting perfectly complements the innovative 10-course tasting menu, where every dish is a work of art—from golden glazed swede with citrus marmalade to BBQ Maitake d'Été. The brioche croissant with pesto dipping sauce is unforgettable. Impeccable service, exquisite wine pairings, and thoughtful touches make it perfect for special occasions. A must-visit culinary experience! Obviously, not cheap, but well worth it.

What do you like most about living in London?

London is a feast for the senses. From indulging in Michelin-starred meals to grabbing street food at Borough Market, the city's culinary scene is unmatched. Its museums and theatres bring culture to life, while vibrant neighbourhoods like Soho and Shoreditch buzz with energy. Whether it's rooftop cocktails, live music, or late-night chatter in a cozy pub, London always brings it home."

Made or Born Londoner?

> *I was born in Peru but moved to London when I married an English man. I still feel Lima is my home, but London is a very honorable second. Followed by Madrid."*

What do you like most about living in London?

> *London brings the world together. Strolling its neighborhoods is a journey across vibrant markets, festivals, and countless languages. From savoring global cuisines in Soho to celebrating Diwali on Trafalgar Square, all cultures here are woven into one thriving tapestry."*

My secret to happiness:

"Can't say, but it runs on a rechargeable battery and it's not my phone!"

María Fernanda

Stay-at-home mom

— Born in Peru, now based in London, recommends...

Secret Spot
— The Canary Wharf Art Trail

This is London's largest outdoor public art collection with over 100 sculptures and installations. From towering contemporary pieces to intricate architectural art. Essentially an open-air museum. Highlights include thought-provoking works by renowned artists and serene spots perfect for reflection. It's a vibrant yet peaceful escape, blending art with urban energy.

Favorite Pub
— Duke on the Green

235 New Kings Rd, SW6 3BN

The Duke on the Green is a gem overlooking Parsons Green, perfect for any occasion. With its warm orange décor and dog-friendly vibe, it's inviting to locals and visitors alike. The food is fantastic—don't miss the fish and chips or Sunday roast! The mix of classic pub charm and lively energy makes it ideal for lazy lunches or buzzing weekend gatherings.

Favorite Restaurant
— Señor Ceviche

Kingly Court, Carnaby, W1B 5PW

Señor Ceviche is a vibrant slice of Lima in London, serving some of the best Peruvian food around. The ceviche is a standout—fresh, zesty, and packed with flavor—while the anticuchos (chargrilled skewers) and creative small plates hit every spot. The open kitchen adds energy, and the Pisco cocktails, especially the chilli Pisco Sour, are a must-try. With friendly service, a buzzing atmosphere, and authentic Peruvian flair, it's my perfect and yummy night out. Remember, I'm Peruvian, and this is the real deal.

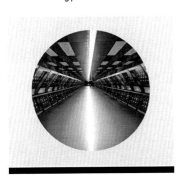

My secret to happiness:

"Going to bed with a clean conscience."

Nick Yates

Civil Engineer

— Born and raised in London, recommends...

Made or Born Londoner?

> *I wish I had an exotic story about being born elswhere and moving to London to chase a sexy professional dream! I don't. Garden variety London lad.*

🔒 Secret Spot
— *Outernet*

Outernet London is a jaw-dropping experience like no other! Located near Tottenham Court Road, its massive Ultra HD screens create an immersive, futuristic world right in the heart of the city. Free to visit, the visuals are stunning, blending art and tech seamlessly. Whether you're passing by or staying to explore, Outernet is a must-see marvel that redefines entertainment.

🍸 Favorite Pub
— *The Ship & Shovell*

2 Craven Passage, WC2N 5NF

The Ship & Shovell near Charing Cross is a unique pub split across two buildings, connected underground by a tunnel. Its cozy, traditional English charm pairs perfectly with Badger Beers and hearty pub food like fish and chips or cheeseburgers. With friendly staff and a welcoming atmosphere, it's a standout spot for an authentic British pub experience.

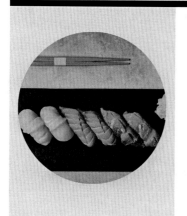

🍴 Favorite Restaurant
— *Sumi*

157 Westbourne Grove, W11 2RS

This restaurant is the little sister to Endo Kazutoshi's Michelin-starred Endo at the Rotunda. The refined menu draws from Japanese traditions with global influences. Highlights include melt-in-your-mouth scallops, perfectly seasoned seafood rice, creamy matcha cake, and unforgettable mushroom miso. With warmth, elegance and a friendly staff, this is a culinary gem.

> *I love London's seamless blend of history and modernity. Ancient landmarks like the Tower of London stand proudly beside sleek skyscrapers like The Shard, creating a city where tradition and innovation coexist.*

What do you like most about living in London?

My secret to happiness:

"Spending time facing the sea to find my peace."

Malika

Biochemist

— Born and bred in London, recommends...

Made or Born a Londoner?

My parents moved to the UK from Nigeria before my siblings and I were born. I grew up in North London, but have been living in southeasth London for ten years."

Secret Spot
— The Courtauld Gallery

If you love art, you'll "sniff" the Courtauld Gallery like a narcotic. It's a cozy, stunning space filled with treasures like Van Gogh's *Self-Portrait with Bandaged Ear*. Wandering through its historic rooms feels like a personal journey through timeless masterpieces. Conveniently located at Somerset House, it's a short walk from Covent Garden or Temple Station.

Favorite Pub
— The Chapel Market Tarven

58 Penton St, N1 9PZ

The Chapel Market Tavern is a lively spot brimming with character. Tucked into the bustling street market, it blends a warm, old-school pub vibe with inventive food and a stellar beer selection. Try their rotating craft ales—they're always on point. The friendly atmosphere makes it perfect for unwinding after exploring Islington.

Favorite Restaurant
— Hot Stone

9 Chapel Market, N1 9EZMa

An unforgettable dining experience where you get to cook premium cuts of wagyu or even certified Kobe beef right at your table on sizzling hot stones. Their sushi and sashimi are top-tier—the seared salmon with truffle is pure indulgence. The space is intimate, perfect for a special night out, and the staff make the whole experience feel personal and fun.

What do you like most about living in London?

I love London because no one ever asks where you're from— it's just understood that being a Londoner means being from "somewhere else". The only identity that matters here is being cool, and I feel free to be unapologetically myself."

Made or Born Londoner?

> *My parents were students in London when they met who loved it so much they decided to stay. My father is French Canadian and my mother is Lebanese."*

🔒 Secret Spot
— *Francis Road*

Recently ranked by *Time Out* as one of the coolest neighborhoods in the world, Leyton is home to my secret spot: Francis Road. This charming stretch is a true community hub—no chains, just independent stores, cozy cafes, and a rare sense of togetherness. You'll discover artisan bakeries, quirky gift shops, and friendly locals. It's the perfect place to enjoy a relaxed, village-like atmosphere and see an authentic slice of London.

🔑 Favorite Pub
— *The Leyton Star*

16 High Rd., E15 2BX

A welcoming pub in the coolest neighborhood in London with incredible staff who go above and beyond. They keep things running smoothly even during busy events like England games. The space is spacious, air-conditioned, with a lovely beer garden. A proper sports bar with great food—burgers and fries are delicious. Perfect for chilling with friends, catching a game, or even hosting an event!

> My secret to happiness:
>
> *"A delicious burger, an ice-cold beer on a sunny day."*

Patrick Reese

Real Estate Developer

— Born in Montreal, now based in London, recommends...

What do you like most about living in London?

> *I love London for its multi-textured aesthetics. One moment, you're wandering through the gritty charm of Leyton in East London, buzzing with creativity and street art. Then, you're transported to the serene, leafy elegance of Chelsea, with its refined streets and upscale vibe. A quick hop takes you to Brick Lane, bursting with culture, spices, and a vibrant community. London's patchwork of contrasts—raw and polished, old and new—creates an endlessly fascinating city where every turn tells a different story."*

Favorite Restaurant
— *Burnt Smokehouse*

161a Midland Rd, E10 6JT

Only in London will you find a halal Texan BBQ smokehouse, featuring the culinary genius of a Romanian American! Burnt Smokehouse in Leyton is a dream for BBQ lovers and a favorite in the local South Asian community. The brisket is unbelievably tender, packed with smoky flavor, and the smash burger? Absolute perfection with crispy edges and a juicy center. The chicken-fat fries and lamb ribs are standouts, while the coleslaw adds a refreshing touch. Friendly staff and the unlicensed, BYOB vibe add to the charm. Arrive early to beat the queue—it's worth it!

Favorite Restaurant
— *Kolamba*

Made or Born Londoner?

> *I was born in Dubai to Sri Lankan parents who immigrated to the UK. I moved to London to study and never left."*

🔒 Secret Spot
— *Phoenix Garden*

The Phoenix Garden near Covent Garden is my little sanctuary. It's tucked away, quiet, and feels worlds apart from the madness of the West End. I love sitting there with a coffee, surrounded by wildflowers and buzzing bees, soaking in the calm. It's not polished or manicured—it's charmingly rugged, a true hidden gem for when you need a breather from London's fast pace.

🍷 Favorite Pub
— *The Spaniard's Inn*

Spaniards Rd, NW3 7JJ

This pub in Hampstead dates back to the 1500s and is steeped in legends, from highwaymen like Dick Turpin to literary greats like Keats and Dickens. The beer garden is stunning, especially in the summer, with views over Hampstead Heath. I love stopping by for a Sunday roast after a long walk through the Heath; their Yorkshire puddings are massive, and the gravy is spot on.

My secret to happiness:

"A good book, a glass of wine, and a hot blanket!"

Sonia De Alwis

Physician

— *Born in Dubai, raised in Birmingham, now based in London, recommends...*

What do you like most about living in London?

> *Growing up in Birmingham, I thought I knew diversity, but here it's on another level. You can explore the food, culture, and traditions of a dozen countries in a single day. After Dubai's glitz and Birmingham's warmth, London feels like the perfect middle ground—cosmopolitan but grounded."*

🍴 Favorite Restaurant
— *Kolamba*

21 Kingly St, W1B 5QA

Most people know Indian food, but have you tried Sri Lankan cuisine? This Soho spot will win you over. The cozy vibe, warm decor, and spice-filled aroma draw you in. The black pork curry is outstanding, egg hoppers are perfect for sharing, and the glazed bacon is unforgettable. Don't miss the yellow monkfish curry, devilled king prawns, or spicy dry-fried beef with chili and tomato. The friendly staff add to the charm. After one visit, you'll be hooked—and telling everyone about it!

PUBLIC SUBWAY

The London Underground.
The city's beating heart.

My secret to happiness:

"Remembering that someone, somewhere has it worse off."

Sophia Tariq

Sustainable Architect

— Born in Birmingham raised in London, recommends...

🍴 Favorite Restaurant
— *Gunpowder*

11 White's Row, Spitalfields, E1 7NF

Gunpowder in Spitalfields serves up Indian dishes with a creative twist. The ambiance is cozy and intimate, making it perfect for a relaxed meal. Their Kashmiri lamb chops are unforgettable—tender, perfectly spiced, and full of flavor. The spicy venison and vermicelli doughnut is another standout. Prices are fair, and the service strikes that perfect balance of friendly and professional. It's an excellent choice for both casual dinners and special occasions. This is part of a small chain, but don't let that put you off. Each chain has its own DNA and there is nothing formulaic here.

Made or Born Londoner?

❝ *My parents immigrated from Pakistan in the 1980s, and I grew up in Birmingham. I moved to London for university and stayed—I just couldn't leave the buzz."*

🔒 Secret Spot
— *Hackney Marshes*

I love Hackney Marshes—it's like a countryside escape right here in the city. You can hear birds instead of traffic and watch the River Lea meander by. There's something grounding about the wild, untamed feel of the place, with sprawling fields and hidden paths perfect for a walk or a quiet moment. I like bringing a coffee and sketchpad to draw the wildflowers, but it's also great for spotting wildlife or just clearing your head after a chaotic week.

🍷 Favorite Pub
— *Pembury Tavern*

90 Amhurst Road, E8 1JH

This is a true neighborhood haunt. The atmosphere is always relaxed, with plenty of space to breathe even when it's buzzing. Their house-brewed beers are a treat, especially paired with one of their incredible wood-fired pizzas—crispy, cheesy perfection. The staff are friendly, and the place always feels welcoming, whether I'm there with friends or just enjoying some time alone. It's the kind of pub where you can lose track of time.

What do you like most about living in London?

❝ *As an architect, I love how London layers centuries of history into one skyline. Walking past the Shard and St. Paul's within minutes is thrilling. I'm fascinated by the city's hidden details—Victorian shopfronts, quirky alleyways—that reveal the stories behind this ever-evolving metropolis."*

Favorite Restaurant
— *Gunpowder*

My secret to happiness:

"Always finishing what I start."

Liam Abbot

Freelance Journalist

— Born in Brighton, now based in London, recommends...

Made or Born Londoner?

" *I grew up in Brighton but moved to London at 22 to chase my dream of becoming a journalist. I stayed for the stories, the food, and the people."*

🔒 Secret Spot
— Netil360

This rooftop above Netil Market is tucked away, with a view of East London that feels perfectly unpolished. I grab a coffee from the market below, sit with my notebook, and just soak it all in. On sunny days, you can spot people lounging or chatting with the city buzzing faintly in the background. It's one of those places that reminds me why I fell in love with London—calm but still alive, raw but beautiful.

🍷 Favorite Pub
— The Camel

277 Globe Rd, E2 0JE

This pub is everything I want in a local. It's small but cozy, and the pies? Unreal. They're proper homemade, not the reheated stuff you get elsewhere. The drinks list is simple but good, and there's always this warm, welcoming atmosphere. On a rainy evening, it's like a little slice of home. Plus, you'll always find a mix of locals and friendly faces—it feels like the heart of the neighborhood.

🍴 Favorite Restaurant
— Tayyabs

83-89 Fieldgate St, E1 1JU

I've probably been to Tayyabs more times than I can count. The lamb chops are legendary—charred, smoky, and so flavorful—and the curries have this rich, vibrant depth. It's always busy, which adds to the buzz, and the prices are ridiculously good for the quality. Their freshly made naan is pillowy perfection, perfect for scooping up every drop of curry. The energy here feels like a celebration—every meal is an event. Even waiting in line feels worth it when the food arrives. It's the kind of place that stays with you long after the meal.

What do you like most about living in London?

" *London is an endless feast for me. It celebrates every culture through its food—one night, I'm at a Malaysian supper club; the next, I'm hunting down the best bagels in Whitechapel. The city's layers of history and the people who make it their own inspire my writing. There's always a new flavor, a new story, or a fresh perspective waiting around the corner."*

Made or Born a Londoner?

I grew up in Lagos and moved to London with my family at 14. After university, I stayed for the opportunities and cultural richness."

Secret Spot
— Japan Centre

Hidden in plain sight near the buzz of Leicester Square, this is a treasure trove for lovers of Japanese culture. Wander through aisles packed with imported snacks, freshly made sushi, and artisanal sake. Their grab-and-go bento boxes are perfect for enjoying at nearby St. James's Park or Trafalgar Square. Tucked within its corners, you'll also find unique Japanese ceramics, kitchenware, and books, making it feel like a mini Tokyo right in the heart of London.

Favorite Pub
— The Ivy House

40 Stuart Rd, SE15 3BE

This isn't your typical pub—it's community-owned and has a real heart. The live music nights are my favorite; you can feel the passion of the performers. They serve solid, no-fuss pub food, and there's a big, welcoming mix of people. It's not about fancy frills, just good vibes and great company.

My secret to happiness:

"Planting seeds of goods in the students I teach."

Amara Eze

School Teacher

— Born in Lagos, now lives in London, recommends...

What do you like most about living in London?

I love London's constant conversation between past and present. As someone who teaches history, I'm in awe of how it surrounds you—from Roman ruins to brutalist estates. But it's the city's stories that really inspire me: the immigrant families, the creative rebels, the quiet changemakers. London is a living archive, and I feel lucky to be part of its story."

Favorite Restaurant
— Chishuru

9 Market Row, SW9 8LB

Chishuru in Brixton offers a refined take on West African cuisine, blending traditional flavors with modern techniques. The tasting menu is a journey through bold, vibrant dishes that remind me of home but with a contemporary twist. Their goat shoulder is tender and packed with flavor, and the plantain is cooked to perfection. The intimate setting and attentive service make it perfect for special occasions or when you want to treat yourself. Plus, the chef is always experimenting, so there's something new every time.

Favorite Restaurant
— *Hostaria Da Corrado*

Made or Born Londoner?

" *I moved from Ahmedabad for university and stayed for the career opportunities— and the endless distractions that London offers away from the laptop.*"

What do you like most about living in London?

" *London's pace keeps me on my toes. It's a city that doesn't stop, and I love that energy. My favorite thing is its contrasts— one moment, you're in the middle of a fast-paced tech district, and the next, you're on a quiet canal walk. It's that blend of chaos and calm that makes it special.*"

🔒 Secret Spot
— *Ropemakers Fields*

There's this tiny park near Limehouse Basin called Ropemakers Fields. It's quiet, tucked away, and has the most incredible view of the boats in the basin. I go there to clear my head or just sit and watch the light change on the water. It's my little escape from the craziness of Canary Wharf.

🍷 Favorite Pub
— *The Grapes*

76 Narrow St, E14 8BP

This is one of London's oldest pubs, and you can feel the history in its wooden beams and riverside views. The beer selection is solid, but honestly, it's the charm of sitting on the deck, watching the Thames roll by, that keeps me coming back. A pint here feels like stepping into a different era.

My secret to happiness:

"Switch off your phone and look up."

Arjun Patel

Software Engineer

— *Born in Ahmedabad, now lives in London, recommends...*

🍴 Favorite Restaurant
— *Hawksmoor Wood Wharf*

1 Water St, Wood Wharf, E14 5GX

Hawksmoor in Wood Wharf is the haven for next-level perfectly cooked, beautifully seasoned steak. The triple-cooked chips are ridiculously good. It's pricey, but you get what you pay for. The waterfront setting at Wood Wharf adds something extra, especially at sunset. Service is always top-notch without being stuffy, and the sticky toffee pudding is a must to finish off.

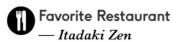

My secret to happiness:

"Taking time out to do something for me, even if it's a pat on the back."

Ella Hughes

Illustrator/Mural Artist

— Born in Bristol, now based in London, recommends...

🍴 Favorite Restaurant
— Itadaki Zen

139 King's Cross Rd, WC1X 9BJ

Itadaki Zen is a serene vegan Japanese restaurant near King's Cross that feels like stepping into another world. The focus is on simple, elegant dishes, with the sushi and tempura being standouts. Their ethos of combining food and mindfulness is something I love—every bite feels intentional. The atmosphere is calm and understated, perfect for a peaceful evening. It's a great spot when you're craving something healthy, satisfying, and beautifully presented.

What do you like most about living in London?

> *It's like a giant sketchbook—its streets, people, and chaos constantly inspire. I love walking* through Shoreditch and seeing how street art evolves almost daily. It's a conversation of color and ideas, and I always feel part of it. Even when I'm burnt out, the city has a way of reigniting something in me."

Made or Born Londoner?

> *I grew up in Bristol and moved here in my 20s for art school. I stayed because London always pushes me creatively—it's electric."*

🔒 Secret Spot
— Kentish Town

This neighborhood is full of architectural treasures, and Kelly Street is a favorite. Just off Kentish Town Road, its pastel-colored, Grade II-listed terraces feel like a quiet retreat from the bustle. Nearby streets like Little Green Street and Quadrant Grove add even more charm, making it perfect for a peaceful, inspiring stroll. It's the kind of area where you'll want to slow down and take in every detail.

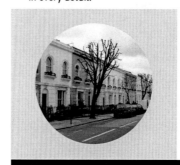

🍷 Favorite Pub
— The Hawley Arms

2 Castlehaven Rd, NW1 8QU

This pub has serious character—there's always something happening. The rooftop terrace is my favorite spot, especially in the summer with a cold cider. Inside, it's got this indie vibe with old gig posters and a buzz that feels quintessentially Camden. A pint here after a day of sketching? Bliss.

Made or Born Londoner?

> *I grew up in Amman and came to London for my master's degree. The city's history and innovation drew me in."*

🔒 Secret Spot
— *Potters Fields Park*

There's a bench by the river in Potters Fields Park, just past Tower Bridge. It's nothing fancy, but the view of the bridge and the river, especially at dusk, is stunning. It's my thinking spot when I need to clear my head or find inspiration. Sometimes the simplest places are the best.

🍷 Favorite Pub
— *The George*

75 Borough High St, SE1 1NH

This isn't just a pub—it's a piece of history. The George Inn dates back centuries, and you can feel the stories in its timbered walls. The courtyard is a great spot to unwind with a pint, and the food's surprisingly good for such a historic place. It's like stepping into old London while enjoying the comforts of today.

My secret to happiness:
"Never saying things I will regret or need to apologize for."

Omar Al-Masri

Civil Engineer

— *Born and Amman, now based in London, recommends...*

What do you like most about living in London?

> *I love how its infrastructure tells a story— Victorian railway bridges side by side with sleek glass* skyscrapers. *I love how the city keeps evolving while honoring its past. There's also a focus on sustainability, which inspires me to push boundaries in my own work."*

🍴 Favorite Restaurant
—*Arabica Borough Market*

3 Rochester Walk, SE1 9AF

Arabica brings the flavors of the Levant to London in the best way. Their mezze is unbeatable—creamy hummus, smoky baba ghanoush, and fresh tabbouleh. The lamb shoulder melts in your mouth, and the saffron rice is perfection. The restaurant started as a small stall in Borough Market, growing into this vibrant, modern space while keeping its authentic charm. Its location in the heart of the market makes every visit feel connected to London's culinary heartbeat. The open kitchen adds to the buzz, letting you see the dishes come alive. It's the perfect spot for a relaxed yet memorable meal with friends.

My secret to happiness!

"To see the world as it really is, not through my biased lens."

Emma Larsen

Photographer

— *Born in Copenhagen, recommends...*

🍴 Favorite Restaurant
— *Pizarro*

194 Bermondsey St, SE1 3TQ

Pizarro is where food meets art. The jamón croquetas are like little edible sculptures, and the octopus? It's a masterpiece on a plate. The space has these huge windows that flood the room with light—it's like dining in a gallery. Sharing tapas with friends here feels like painting with flavors—creative, fun, and just a little indulgent. The service is warm and effortless, adding to the charm. It's the kind of place where you lose track of time in the best way.

Made or Born Londoner?

🔒 Secret Spot
— *Thames Path*

The Thames Path is my little sanctuary. There's a stretch near Bermondsey where the city feels slower, almost reflective. I love walking there with my camera—it's perfect for capturing unexpected angles of London's skyline or just watching the water catch the light. Sometimes I sit on a bench and sketch, letting the sounds of the river drown out the noise of the day. It's where I go to recharge and reconnect.

What do you like most about living in London?

> *I grew up in Copenhagen and came to London to study photography. The city's energy and diversity make it the perfect playground."*

🍺 Favorite Pub
— *The Woolpack*

98 Bermondsey St, SE1 3UB

This may be the best pub in south London. The beer garden is perfect for flipping through my photos on a sunny afternoon. Their craft beers are a little adventure in a glass. The vibe is effortlessly cool, with fairy lights and that buzz of creative chatter all around. Plus, their wood-fired pizzas—don't get me started! It's where I go to let the day settle.

> *I love exploring London's hidden alleyways, catching golden hour light bouncing off brick walls, or finding a rooftop with a killer view. There's always something to capture here. Plus, the creative freedom and mix of people make it feel like there's always a story waiting to told and retold."*

Favorite Restaurant
— *Pizarro*

My secret to happiness:

"Pour your heart into your craft, and don't forget dessert."

Luca Bernardi

Pastry Chef

— Born in Florency, now lives in London, recommends...

Made or Born a Londoner?

" *I moved from Florence for a culinary apprenticeship and never left. London's food scene is so exciting—it's a playground for any chef.*"

🔒 Secret Spot
— *Gelatorino*

This gelateria is tucked away in Covent Garden, you could almost miss it, but their gelato is an art form. The pistachio and hazelnut flavors transport me straight to Italy. I love watching them churn it fresh in the traditional way—it's mesmerizing. Whenever I need a taste of home, I grab a scoop, wander through the cobbled streets, and suddenly, London feels even more magical. When an Italian recommends a gelateria in London, pay attention!

🍷 Favorite Pub
— *The Windsor Castle*

114 Campden Hill Rd, W8 7AR

I celebrated my first big promotion as a pastry chef here. We crammed into those tiny, cozy nooks, and the owner brought over a celebratory pint on the house. The beer garden, with its fairy lights, is my escape when the kitchen gets too intense. Their Sunday roast feels like a warm hug after a long week—it keeps me coming back. Things that keep me coming back.

🍴 Favorite Restaurant
— *Core by Clare Smyth*

92 Kensington Park Rd, W11 2PN

Art meets food here. This three-Michelin-starred restaurant offers tasting menus. Every dish is a story unfolding. The potato and roe is a masterpiece of simplicity and flavor, and the desserts are my kind of heaven. With an elegant dining room, service is flawless and unpretentious. Expensive but worth every penny!

What do you like most about living in London?

" *London is a city of reinvention. You can be whoever you want here, and the food reflects that—it's a mashup of cultures and flavors. I love how you can start your day with an English breakfast, have sushi for lunch, and finish with a plate of pasta that tastes just like home. For me, the city feels like an endless buffet of creativity and opportunity.*"

Made or Born Londoner?

> *I grew up in Edinburgh and moved to London to teach. The city's diversity makes every day feel like an adventure."*

🔒 Secret Spot
— *Backstory*

There's a tiny independent bookstore in Balham called Backstory. It's small but full of charm, with a brilliantly curated selection of books. I love browsing for new reads, especially in the children's section—it inspires my lesson plans. The staff are lovely and always recommend something unexpected. It's my go-to for quiet, inspiring moments.

🍷 Favorite Pub
— *The Sun*

47 Old Town, SW4 0JL

My secret to happiness:

"The perfect book or a sunny afternoon."

This has everything you want in a pub—cozy but with enough space to breathe. The garden is magical in the summer, with fairy lights and a view of Clapham Old Town. The staff make everyone feel at home, and their Sunday roast is the highlight of my week—the gravy alone is worth the visit. It's got that perfect mix of lively chatter and laid-back vibes.

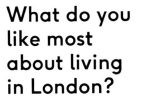

Holly McAllister

Primary School Teacher

— Born in Edinbrugh, now lives in London recommends...

What do you like most about living in London?

> *London is a place where you never stop learning. I love seeing my students thrive in such a vibrant, multicultural city. For me, the real magic transpires in the parks—you can always find a green space to relax or play."*

🍴 Favorite Restaurant
— *Minnow*

21 The Pavement, SW4 0HY

Minnow is a little slice of magic. Founded by husband-and-wife team Chris Frichot and Saba Tsegaye, their seasonal menu is always exciting—I can't resist the sea bass with saffron potatoes when it's on. The interior is charming, with floral touches that make it feel so welcoming. The service is attentive without being overbearing, and it's affordable enough to visit regularly. It's my happy place for a relaxed dinner or weekend brunch.

**Favorite
Restaurant**
— *Ottolenghi
Islington*

Made or Born Londoner?

❝ *I was born in Cairo and moved to London for art school. The city's creativity and energy have kept me here ever since.*❞

What do you like most about living in London?

❝ *London is a mosaic of ideas. I love how every neighborhood has its own visual identity— from the bold graffiti of Shoreditch to the elegant shopfronts of Mayfair. The contrast inspires me every day, and the city always feels like it's moving forward.*❞

My secret to happiness:

"Anything made of chocolate."

Yasmin Ahmed

Graphic Designer

— *Born in Cairo, now based in London, recommends...*

🔒 Secret Spot
— *Battlebridge Basin*

A little space tucked behind the London Canal Museum in King's Cross. It's quiet and green, with benches where you can sit and watch the narrowboats drift by. I love taking my sketchpad there— it's a perfect escape when I need a break but don't want to go far from the buzz of the city. Afterward, I usually head to Coal Drops Yard, just a short walk away, for a coffee at Redemption Roasters or a bite at Caravan—it's the perfect way to round out a peaceful afternoon.

🍷 Favorite Pub
— *The Drapers Arms*
44 Barnsbury St, N1 1ER

This pub is as charming as it gets. I'm not much of a drinker, but I love coming here with friends who are. The Sunday roasts are incredible— perfectly cooked and hearty without being heavy. The garden is a lovely spot to soak up the summer vibe while everyone else enjoys a pint. Whether it's a quiet catch-up or a long, relaxed dinner, it always delivers.

🍴 Favorite Restaurant
— *Ottolenghi Islington*
287 Upper St, N1 2TZ

Ottolenghi is an explosion of flavor and color. Their salads are famous for a reason—vibrant, creative, and perfectly balanced. The roasted aubergine with tahini is a personal favorite, and their pastries? Absolutely heavenly. As a Middle Easterner, this is where I come to get my hummus fix. The space itself is bright and airy, with a laid-back yet elegant vibe. It's a little pricey, but the food feels like art on a plate, making it worth every penny.

St. Paul's Cathederal,
London, 7.15 am

81

My secret to happiness:

"Not thinking about it too much."

Henry

Entrepreneur

— Born in the UK and based in London, recommends...

Made or Born Londoner?

❝ *I moved to London when I was 21 and lived there for over 30 years."*

🔒 Secret Spot — *Waterloo Millennium Green*

Grabbing lunch from the fabulous Thai noodle stand on Lower Marsh and taking it to a bench in Waterloo Millennium Green is my little ritual. It's not glamorous—just a park, a bench, and noodles—but it's my London, a simple escape in the middle of the city's buzz.

🍷 Favorite Pub — *The White Hart*

29 Cornwall Rd, Greater, SE1 8TJ

This is a proper pub with proper beer, a great atmosphere, and friendly faces. I usually go for a pint of London Pride, but I'm always tempted by their specials. Near Waterloo, it blends old-school charm with the buzz of theatre-goers from the South Bank.

What do you like most about living in London?

❝ *The sheer number of things going on—it's a city that never stops. There's always an art exhibition to discover, a new restaurant or market to explore, or a new play or art exhibition. The business scene is also dynamic and buzzing with opportunities."*

Favorite Restaurant —*José Tapas Bar*

104 Bermondsey St, SE1 3UB

The José Tapas Bar on Bermondsey Street is small, buzzing, and always worth the wait. They don't take bookings, but that's part of the charm. Squeeze in if you can—the croquetas are dreamy, the jamón melts in your mouth, and the vibe feels like a little slice of Spain right in London. Pair it with a glass of sherry and watch the chefs work their magic in the open kitchen. It's the kind of place where time slows down, and every bite feels like a celebration.

My secret to happiness:

"Being irreverant when I am expected to be docile."

Charlotte King

Architect

— Born in and bred in London, recommends...

Made or Born a Londoner?

" *Born and bred in West London. I've lived in Fulham most of my life—it's the perfect mix of charm and convenience."*

🔓 Secret Spot
— Bookseller's Row

Bookseller's Row on Cecil Court in Covent Garden is a paradise for book lovers. It's a charming little alley lined with independent bookshops, each one a treasure trove of rare editions, vintage prints, and beautifully illustrated maps. There's something magical about the quiet hum of discovery there—stories practically seep from the walls. It's my favorite spot to escape the rush and lose myself in history, words, and imagination.

🍷 Favorite Pub
— The Fulham Arms

8 Fulham Rd, SW6 4EF

This pub feels like home—a little stylish, but not pretentious. The drinks menu is great, and if you are not a huge drinker (shame on you!), the mocktails are spot on. The best part is the people—you always run into someone interesting, eccentric, or mad. Their Scotch eggs are legendary, and the atmosphere? Perfectly cozy with just the right buzz to spark great conversations.

🍴 Favorite Restaurant
— Jugemu

3 Winnett St, W1D 6JY

Jugemu is a slice of Japan in Soho. Rustic and understated. Their okonomiyaki and soba are a revelation—flavors you don't often find in London. The staff are welcoming and happy to explain the menu if you're unsure. It's authentic but not overly polished, and that's what makes it so special. Perfect for a quiet night with amazing food.

What do you like most about living in London?

" *London is like a giant mood board for me. The layers of architecture, the bold new builds alongside centuries-old townhouses, inspire everything I do. I love walking through neighborhoods and catching snippets of different lives—an artist's studio here, a grand hotel there. There's no city quite like it for finding beauty in unexpected corners."*

Made or Born Londoner?

> *Born and raised in London, with roots in East London's Hackney. This city shaped the soundtrack of my life."*

🔒 Secret Spot — *Stranger Than Paradise*

There's a vinyl store in Hackney. It is a haven for crate diggers like me—rare finds, obscure records, and a friendly crew who actually know their music. I've lost whole afternoons there, flipping through stacks and discovering sounds I'd never even heard of. It's not just a shop; it's a journey. A must-visit if you want to dig deeper into London's pop culture roots.

🍾 Favorite Pub — *The Shacklewell Arms*

71 Shacklewell Ln, E8 2EB

This pub is pure Dalston, a mix of creative misfits and old-school charm. It's scruffy in the best way, with live music that hits hard and cheap drinks that don't break the bank. The gig room in the back has this gritty, underground vibe that I love—it's where I first saw some of my favorite indie bands. If you're into music and good energy, this is the place to be.

My secret to happiness:

"Find your rhythm and dance to it."

Nathan Chen

Musician

— *Born and bred in London, recommends...*

What do you like most about living in London?

> *London has a heartbeat like no other city. The sounds of the streets, the rhythm of the Tube, and the music from every corner—it's impossible not to be inspired."*

🍴 Favorite Restaurant — *My Neighbours The Dumplings*

165 Lower Clapton Rd, E5 8EQ

This place is dumpling heaven. It's small, casual, and everything feels handmade with care. The prawn and pork dumplings are packed with flavor, and their cold sesame noodles are addictive. They've got great cocktails, too—simple but spot-on. The vibe is laid-back, like you're eating at a mate's place, but with insanely good food. Perfect for a chilled night out.

Favorite
Restaurant
— Ariana II

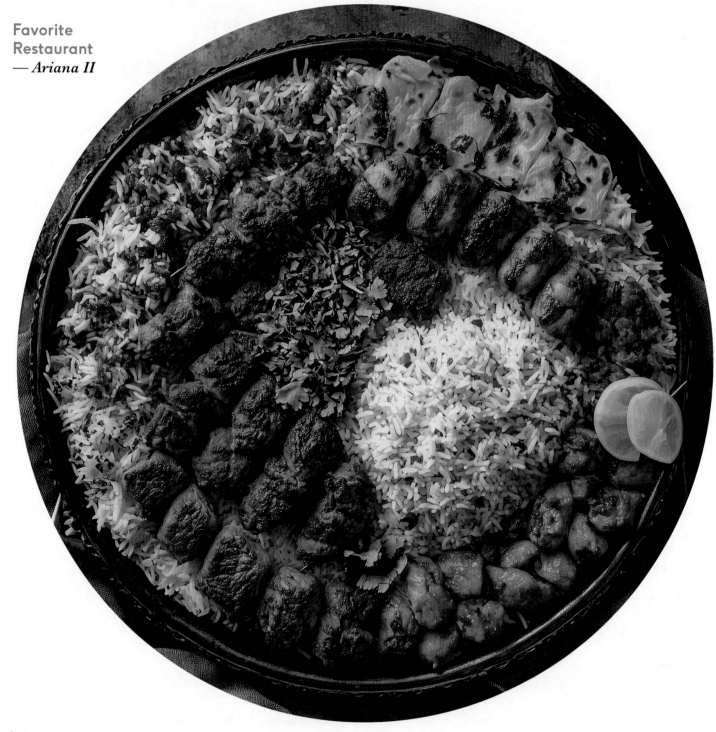

🔒 Secret Spot
— *Kiln Theatre*

This theater in Kilburn is a true cultural hub for the community, shining a spotlight on diverse voices. Their café is perfect for soaking up the creative buzz. The theatre opened in 1980 as the permanent home of the Wakefield Tricycle Company, which built its reputation on British premieres, new writing, children's shows, and community theatre. It's a place where art and stories bring people together.

🍸 Favorite Pub
— *The Black Lion*

295 Kilburn High Rd, NW6 7JR

A gorgeous old Victorian pub in Kilburn with high ceilings and stained-glass windows that make you feel like you've stepped back in time. The crowd is super friendly, and the food is solid—great burgers and even better chips. I love the community vibe; it's a place where everyone feels welcome.

My secret to happiness:

"Give more than I take."

Amara Singh
Charity Worker

— *Born in Leicester, now based in London, recommends...*

Made or Born Londoner?

❝ *I moved from Leicester to study social work at university and stayed to make a difference in the city's diverse communities.*❞

What do you like most about living in London?

❝ *London is a mosaic of cultures, each piece vibrant and essential. The people make this city—so many voices,* experiences, and stories all blending together. For me, it's about connections.*❞

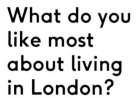

🍴 Favorite Restaurant
— *Ariana II*

241 Kilburn High Rd, NW6 7JN

London's best Afghan restaurant. The lamb qabuli pilaf is tender and full of flavor, and their mantu dumplings are a must-try. The portions are generous, and the prices are super reasonable—it's a warm, family-run spot that always feels inviting. Perfect for when you want something hearty and a bit different.

My secret to happiness:

"Gratitude on steroids."

Kasia Novak

Florist

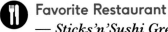

— Born in Kraków, now lives in London, recommends...

🍴 Favorite Restaurant
— Sticks'n'Sushi Greenwich

1 Nelson Rd, SE10 9JB

Sticks'n'Sushi is my guilty pleasure in Greenwich. The presentation is stunning, and the flavors are always on point. Their sashimi is the freshest you'll find, and the yakitori skewers are packed with flavor—I can never pick just one. It's on the pricier side, but for a treat, it's unbeatable. The chic interiors and friendly staff make the experience feel special every time.

Made or Born Londoner?

🔒 Secret Spot
— The Herb Garden - Greenwich Park

There's a hidden herb garden in Greenwich Park, just a short walk from the Observatory. It's small, fragrant, and peaceful, with lavender and rosemary filling the air. I love going there to clear my head or dream up new bouquet designs. Sometimes, I bring a book and stay for hours—it's a secret slice of calm.

What do you like most about living in London?

Born and raised in one of the oldest neighborhoods of ancient Rome, San Lorenzo, which was totally razed during the Second World War. To date, under the Basilica of San Lorenzo, there are bombs yet to be dismantled."

🍷 Favorite Pub
— The Cutty Sark

4-6 Ballast Quay, SE10 9PD

This riverside pub is my sanctuary. It's tucked away in Greenwich and has incredible views of the Thames—perfect for unwinding after a long day arranging flowers. The vibe is relaxed, the fish and chips are crispy perfection, and the cozy interiors make you want to linger. There's something magical about sitting by the river, no matter the season.

London blooms in so many ways. I'm constantly inspired by its parks, markets, and even its weather—it makes flowers all the more special. I love how each neighborhood has its own vibe: from the classic elegance of Kensington to the bohemian charm of Hackney."

Made or Born a Londoner?

> *I moved from Cairns in Australia six years ago to chase a dream of opening a café in Europe's busiest city.*"

🔒 Secret Spot
— *Boundary Rooftop Bar*

This rooftop in Shoreditch is my retreat when I need a moment of peace. You get incredible views of the city skyline, and it's surprisingly quiet during the day. I grab a coffee or a glass of wine, depending on the mood, and just let London spread out in front of me. It's where I come to make peace with whatever may be eating away at me and it always works.

🍷 Favorite Pub
— *The Crown and Shuttle*

226 Shoreditch High St, E1 6PJ

This pub is quintessentially Shoreditch—quirky, friendly, and buzzing. The beer garden is massive, with fairy lights and long wooden tables perfect for meeting up with friends. Their craft beer selection is top-notch, and the staff know their stuff. Top tip: their halloumi fries are the stuff of legends!

My secret to happiness:
"Not fearing failure."

Elliot Matthews
Café Owner

— *Born in Cairns, now based in London, recommends...*

What do you like most about living in London?

> *The café culture here is vibrant but still growing, which makes it exciting to bring Australian coffee traditions into the mix. The changing* seasons, the creative communities, and the way the city comes alive in its own way every day—it's intoxicating. London has become home, but it still keeps me curious.*"

🍴 Favorite Restaurant
— *Smoking Goat*

64 Shoreditch High St, E1 6JJ

Smoking Goat is where I go when I'm craving bold, unforgettable flavors. It's Thai barbecue, but not like you've had before—smoky, spicy, and so satisfying. Their fish sauce wings and the lamb neck massaman curry are absolute standouts. I remember a night when the place was packed, the music was buzzing, and I lost count of how many cocktails and tamarind chicken wings we went through—it was perfect chaos. The vibe is casual but cool, and it's perfect for sharing dishes and a few cocktails with mates. It's Shoreditch in food form.

My secret to happiness:

"To be the master of my own destiny."

Aaron Davis

Tech Entrepreneur

— *Born in San Francisco, now based in London, recommends...*

Made or Born a Londoner?

I moved from San Francisco to expand my startup internationally. London's diversity and energy made it the obvious choice."

🔒 Secret Spot
— *Gabriel's Wharf*

This is my hidden oasis along the Thames. It's got this cool mix of quirky independent shops, little restaurants, and an unbeatable view of the river. I love grabbing a coffee, strolling through the artisan stores, and then just sitting by the water. It's a great spot to slow down and soak up the city without the usual crowds.

🏆 Favorite Pub
— *Anchor Bankside*

34 Park St, SE1 9EF

The Anchor is a piece of history right on the Thames. I love bringing friends here for the riverside terrace—it's unbeatable on a sunny day. I'm not much of a beer guy, but their Pimm's is spot on. The food is great too; their steak and ale pie hits the spot after a long day. It's classic London in all the right ways.

🍴 Favorite Restaurant
— *Flat Iron Borough*

11 Clink Street, SE1 9DG

A steak lover's nirvana near the legendary Borough Market. The menu is simple—just perfectly cooked steak and some sides—but the quality is incredible. The dripping-cooked chips are dangerously good, and the creamed spinach is a must. The vibe is casual but chic, and the prices are surprisingly reasonable for what you're getting. It's one of my favorite places for a laid-back, satisfying dinner.

What do you like most about living in London?

Coming from the States, the history here blows my mind—you can walk past a 300-year-old pub on your way to a cutting-edge tech hub. I also love how international it feels; it's like the world is packed into one city. The creative minds here make it a playground for ideas, and there's always something new to explore."

88

My secret to happiness:

"To chase impossible dreams."

Sofia Alvarez

Documentary Filmmaker

— *Born in Mexico City, now based in London, recommends...*

Made or Born Londoner?

❝ *I moved from Mexico City five years ago for film school and stayed for the endless storytelling opportunities.* ❞

🍷 Favorite Pub
— *Effra Hall Tavern*

38 Kellett Rd, SW2 1EB

In the heart of Brixton, this pub has live jazz nights that make you feel like you're in a movie, and the crowd is always a good mix of locals and visitors. The vibe is unpretentious and full of character—just the way a pub should be. An ice-cold beer, their moorish fries while soaking in the music is just heaven.

🔒 Secret Spot
— *Close-Up Film Centre*

A small, often overlooked cinema in Shoreditch. They screen everything from rare classics to obscure indie films. The vibe is intimate, and the attached library is a goldmine for anyone who loves cinema history. You can spend hours watching films and flipping through old scripts.

🍴 Favorite Restaurant
— *Mestizo Mexican Restaurant*

103 Hampstead Rd, NW1 3EL

If you get tired of fish and chips or pub roasts and start craving some authentic Mexican, Mestizo is the real deal. Their cochinita pibil tacos are packed with flavor, and the chile en nogada is a work of art—sweet, savory, and unforgettable. The space is warm and inviting, with a mezcal bar upstairs that's perfect for a post-dinner drink. It's a bit pricier than your usual taco spot, but the quality and heart in every dish make it more than worth it.

What do you like most about living in London?

❝ *Every street feels like it's hiding a secret, waiting for you to stumble upon it. I love the way Brixton buzzes with life, how a walk along the Southbank feels like stepping into a thousand different worlds, or how you can find poetry in the chaos of rush hour. As a filmmaker, this city constantly surprises me—it's raw, vibrant, and endlessly cinematic. I can't imagine running out of stories to tell here.* ❞

Secret Spot
— *Ropewalk*

Ropewalk at Maltby Street Market is my go-to when I've got a rare morning off. It's tucked under the arches, full of great coffee, craft stalls, and street food. The vibe's proper London—friendly, a bit rough around the edges, but always full of character. I grab a bacon sarnie and wander—it's simple, but it's magic.

Favorite Pub
The Angel

101 Bermondsey Wall E, SE16 4NB

An unbeatable spot right by the Thames. I love sitting outside with a coffee—yeah, I'm not a big drinker—watching the river roll by. It's quiet but still has that lively buzz. Friends rave about the ales, and the food's proper good—fish and chips done right.

My secret to happiness:
"Keep moving, stay curious."

David Carter
Cab Driver

— Born and bred in London recommends...

Made or Born Londoner?

Born and raised in Bermondsey. London isn't just home; it's in my blood. Been driving a black cab here for 30 years."

What do you like most about living in London?

London's like an old friend— always changing, but you know it inside out. I've driven every street, from grand boulevards to tiny alleys, and it never gets boring. What I love most is the city's rhythm—early mornings by the Thames, late nights in Soho, and everything in between. It's the stories you find here that count."

Favorite Restaurant
— *Master Wei Xi'an*

13 Cosmo Pl, WC1N 3AP

Master Wei Xi'an, tucked away in the heart of Bloomsbury, is a rare gem in central London—affordable, unpretentious, and absolutely delicious. Specializing in the rich, bold flavors of Xi'an cuisine, this spot offers dishes like their hand-pulled biang biang noodles and crispy beef pancakes that pack a serious flavor punch. Despite being in such a prime location, the prices are refreshingly reasonable, making it a favorite for anyone craving authentic Chinese food without the hefty bill. It's proof you don't have to break the bank for great food in the city.

Favorite Restaurant
— *The Wolseley*

Made or Born Londoner?

> *I moved to London after university having grown up in Scotland. Both our children are South Londoners born and bred.*

🔒 Secret Spot — *Brockwell Park*

Brockwell Park just south of Brixton. Great views, a secret walled garden, and tonnes of memories. It dates back to the early 19th century when it was part of the Brockwell Hall estate. The land was purchased by London County Council in 1891 to create a public park, preserving its rolling meadows and beautiful views.

♟ Favorite Pub — *The Canton Arms*

177 S Lambeth Rd, SW8 1XP

The Canton Arms on South Lambeth Road is a great local meeting place. The pub has probably been around since the mid 1800s. In 2010, Chef Patron Trish Hilferty took over the establishment and turned it into a proper London gastropub.

My secret to happiness:

"Gardening gloves, a purring cat, family, and friends."

Joanna

Publisher

— *Born in Scotland, now based in London, recommends...*

What do you like most about living in London?

> *The fact that the whole world is on my doorstep. From the Portuguese cafés in Stockwell to the bustling markets in Brixton and the art galleries scattered across the city, there's always something new to discover like finding a little-known bookstore or catching an offbeat play.*

Favorite Restaurant — *The Wolseley*

160 Piccadilly, W1J 9EB

I'm torn between the glamour of The Wolseley and the excitement of whatever the latest opening is in Brixton Market. The Wosley is classic all-day brasserie that's an essential experience for anyone visiting London. It was originally built in 1921 as a grand car showroom before becoming a bank and eventually transforming into a luxury European-style café-restaurant in 2003. Today, it's an iconic part of London's dining scene, celebrated for its elegant Art Deco interiors, impeccable service, and timeless breakfast, lunch, and dinner menus.

"In Richmond's greens, the whispers play, of deer that wander, soft and stray. Beneath the oaks, the quiet hum, Of life at peace where city's numb."

ANONYMOUS

Richmond, 5.15 pm

My secret to happiness:

"Always going to bed dreaming of tomorrow's conquests."

Edward Pennington

Retired Art Dealer

— Born and raised in Rome, recommends...

🔒 Secret Spot
— *The Wallace Collection*

The Wallace Collection in Marylebone is a quiet haven I adore. It's an exquisite gallery of fine art, furniture, and armor, tucked away in a stunning townhouse. The collection is intimate, and the central courtyard café is ideal for a leisurely lunch or coffee. It's a place that feels like a secret, even though it's in plain sight.

🍷 Favorite Pub
— *The Grenadier*

18 Wilton Row, SW1X 7NR

A true London institution, tucked away in a charming mews in Belgravia. It's steeped in history and said to be haunted, though I've yet to encounter any ghosts—just excellent pints and hearty food. Their beef Wellington is superb. I come for the atmosphere: intimate old-world charm.

What do you like most about living in London?

❝ *It's a city of refinement and reinvention. From the regal elegance of St. James's to the avant-garde galleries of Shoreditch, it's a place where the past and future collide beautifully. I adore the theater scene—there's nothing quite like settling into a red velvet chair in Covent Garden and waiting for the curtain to rise.*❞

Made or Born Londoner?

❝ *I was born in Belgravia, a true Londoner through and through.*❞

🍴 Favorite Restaurant
— *Rules*

35 Maiden Ln, WC2E 7LB

Rules is London's oldest restaurant. Stepping inside feels like walking into a Dickens novel. Their game dishes are unparalleled—the roast grouse with bread sauce is a personal favorite. The service is impeccable, and the dark wood-paneled dining room exudes elegance. More than a meal; it's an occasion steeped in tradition.

Favorite Restaurant
— *Rules*

My secret to happiness:

"To never stop learning, even when I feel smug."

Edward

Retired Architect

— Born in the UK, now based in London, recommends...

 Favorite Restaurant
— Villa Bianca

1 Perrin's Ct, NW3 1QS

Villa Bianca has been a Hampstead favorite for decades, and it's easy to see why. Tucked away on a quiet side street, it has this timeless charm that feels like stepping into a different era. The homemade pasta is rich and comforting, and their seafood dishes are always spot-on. The mushroom risotto is unforgettable and the lobster pasta is a masterpiece. The sweetness of the cherry tomatoes balances perfectly with the slight saltiness of the fresh, tender lobster. The family-run atmosphere makes it even more special—you feel like a regular, even if it's your first visit. Perfect for a relaxed dinner with good wine and even better company.

Made or Born Londoner?

" *I moved to London in the 1970s for work, and the city's ever-changing skyline kept me here. I've built a family, a career in London and now see my grandchildren bearing the torch."*

Secret Spot
— The Pergola at Hampstead Hill Gardens

This is one of the city's hidden treasures. It's this slightly crumbling yet stunning structure, surrounded by overgrown plants and offering the most peaceful views. I often bring a book or a paper here—something about the combination of architecture and nature makes it a magical escape.

Favorite Pub
— The Holly Bush

22 Holly Mount, NW3 6SG

The Holly Bush has this warm, welcoming vibe that makes you want to settle in and stay a while. Its cozy oak-paneled interiors and roaring fireplace are perfect for unwinding, especially on a chilly day. The steak and ale pie is always a winner—hearty and full of flavor—and their selection of ales is top-notch. I've had some of the most entertaining, enriching, inspiring, and memorable conversations here and so will you!

What do you like most about living in London?

" *London is a living museum of architecture. Every corner has a story to tell—from the intricate brickwork of Victorian terraces to the sweeping curves of the Barbican. It's a city that layers its history with constant innovation. Walking through London is like flipping through centuries of design, and for me, it's endlessly inspiring."*

Made or Born Londoner?

🔒 Secret Spot
— *Chelsea Physic Garden*

This historic botanical garden is nestled along the Thames, filled with medicinal plants, rare herbs, and beautiful flowers. I love to wander the paths, finding peace and inspiration among the diverse plant life. It's an oasis in the middle of the city, and it feels like a secret garden that's been there for centuries. It's the perfect spot to recharge and let creativity flow.

> *I was born in Tokyo and grew up in London—my mum's Japanese and my dad's English. I love both cities with equal passion!"*

💡 Favorite Pub
— *The Cross Keys*

119 King's Rd, SW3 4PL

This my local pub and is the perfect mix of chic and cozy. The interiors are charming without being overdone, and they've got a great wine list—not something you expect from a pub! Their crispy squid is a must, and the garden seating is ideal for a quiet drink on a sunny day. It's Chelsea elegance with a laid-back twist.

My secret to happiness:

"Loving all the parts of me. The good, the bad, and the ugly!"

Aiko

Fashion Editor

— *Born in Tokyo, seduced by London, recommends...*

What do you like most about living in London?

> *London is where cultures collide in the best way. As someone who's grown up between two worlds, I love how this* city feels like a tapestry of styles, traditions, and ideas. It celebrates contrasts and makes them beautiful. For the wellbeing of my soul, there's nowhere more inspiring."

🍴 Favorite Restaurant
— *Dinings SW3*

Lennox Gardens Mews, SW3 2JH

Dinings SW3 is where I go for sushi that feels like an art form. Their wagyu beef sushi and sea bass carpaccio are incredible—delicate, fresh, and full of flavor. The intimate atmosphere and hidden location make it feel like a secret discovery. The omakase experience here is unforgettable, with each dish crafted to perfection and paired expertly with sake. It's a little pricey, but for a special night out, it's worth every penny. The staff are attentive without being intrusive, adding to the sense of refined luxury.

Favorite Restaurant
— *Rogues*

Made or Born Londoner?

> *I moved from Dublin six years ago for a few steady gigs, and London's food scene has kept me inspired ever since. And before you ask, no, I don't think AI will render my profession obsolete."*

🔒 Secret Spot — *Chinese Pagoda*

There's a hidden corner at Victoria Park called the Chinese Pagoda. It's tucked away near the canal and has this serene vibe that's perfect for clearing your head. On quiet mornings, the reflection of the pagoda in the water is stunning—it's like stepping into a postcard. I'll grab a coffee from a nearby stall and sit on one of the benches, soaking in the calm before heading back into the city chaos.

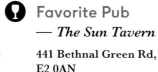
💡 Favorite Pub — *The Sun Tavern*

441 Bethnal Green Rd, E2 0AN

My go-to after a long work day. Old-school charm with exposed brick, low lighting, and just enough bustle to keep it lively. Their whiskey selection is incredible. Once a bartender, convinced me to try their homemade poitín cocktails—absolutely unforgettable. You'll experience a slice of the real East London.

My secret to happiness:
"Not fretting about a secret to happiness!"

Declan Murphy
Freelnace Photographer

— *Born in Dublin, appropriated by London, recommends…*

What do you like most about living in London?

> *When I first moved here I was wandering through Borough Market overwhelmed by the aromas of fresh bread, sizzling chorizo, and spices. I ended up buying a lamb kofta wrap and ate it by the Thames. Experiences like this are what makes you fall hopelessly in love with London."*

🍴 Favorite Restaurant — *Rogues*

460 Hackney Rd, E2 9EG

Rogues is one of those places you almost don't want to share—it's that special. Their seasonal, ever-changing menu always surprises me; I've had dishes here I still dream about, like their slow-cooked lamb with wild garlic or the celeriac with brown butter. The setting is low-key but stylish, with a creative energy that mirrors the food. It's like a little sanctuary of culinary brilliance in Bethnal Green. I've seen household-name British chefs eating there and that says something.

My secret to happiness:

"Never eat alone."

Made or Born Londoner?

" *I grew up in Brighton, but London's food scene drew me here in my twenties, and I've never looked back."*

What do you like most about living in London?

" *London is where food tells a story. Growing up with Greek and Italian roots, I've always been fascinated by how cuisine connects people. Here, you'll find every flavor, every influence."*

Marco Stefanides

Chef

— *Born in Brighton, now based in London, recommends...*

🍴 Favorite Restaurant
— *Josephine Bouchon*

315 Fulham Road, SW10 9QH

This classic neighborhood French place oozes comfort and elegance. Their cassoulet is perfection—rich, hearty, and brimming with flavor—and their tarte Tatin is a dessert I'll never stop ordering. The place itself is stunning, with soft lighting and an intimate feel that makes it ideal for a long, relaxed meal. It's a chef's dream because you can taste the care in every bite. Simple, honest French food.

🍷 Favorite Pub
— *The Windmill*

Clapham Common South Side, SW4 9DE

Sitting on the edge of Clapham Common, this laid-back pub feels a world away from a busy kitchen. I'm partial to their cask ales, and the Sunday roast is top-notch—juicy meat, crispy potatoes, and gravy that could solve world problems. They also have more than 40 beautiful hotel rooms on site.

🔒 Secret Spot
— *Old English Garden*

There's a quiet section of Battersea Park called the Old English Garden. It's tucked away, and its beautifully landscaped flower beds and tranquil pond make it feel like a secret retreat. It's one of my favorite places to sit jot down ideas for new dishes. The air always seems fresher there, and it's a perfect escape from the city's constant buzz.

Made or Born Londoner?

> *I moved here from Rio de Janeiro 20 years ago to teach samba at a cultural festival, and the beat of London stole my heart.*

🔒 Secret Spot
— *Mercato Mayfair*

This place is tucked inside a beautifully restored church. It's not just a market—it's an experience. You can grab incredible food from all over the world, whether it's freshly made pasta or Korean barbecue, and sit beneath the stunning vaulted ceilings. The upstairs wine bar is perfect for a quiet drink, and the whole place has this magical mix of history and modern energy.

🍷 Favorite Pub
— *The World's End*

23 Stroud Green Rd, N4 2DF

I love The World's End because it's always a bit unpredictable. It's the sort of pub where a random guy at the bar can start strumming his guitar, and suddenly the whole place is singing along. Their craft beer is excellent, but it's the laid-back, anything-can-happen vibe that keeps me coming back.

My secret to happiness:

"Dance until your shoes fall off!"

Camila Monteiro

Dance Instructor

— *Born in Rio de Janeiro, now based in London, recommends...*

What do you like most about living in London?

> *London is like a rhythm—it's always pulsating. The diversity reminds me of Brazil; you can find a piece of every culture in this city, and you can curate your own tribe, your own life, just as it suits you. Very few cities do this as well as London.*

🍴 Favorite Restaurant
— *Tarshish*

16-20 High Rd, N22 6BX

Tarshish is a feast for the senses. Their Mediterranean-inspired menu is packed with flavor—I can't resist their lamb chops, and the hummus with lamb is next-level. The two-story space has a modern, vibrant vibe, and the service always feels warm and welcoming.

My secret to happiness:

"My family, my girlfriends, and cheese!"

Didi

Creative Director

— *Grew up in Dulwich, now based in London, recommends...*

Made or Born Londoner?

I grew up in Dulwich, but after university, I couldn't resist returning to London. Its energy, creativity, and endless opportunities have a way of calling you home."

Secret Spot — *John Sandoe Books*

John Sandoe Books in Chelsea is my haven. It's a labyrinth of floor-to-ceiling shelves packed with everything from rare finds to contemporary gems. The staff have a magical ability to recommend exactly what you didn't know you needed. I love spending an afternoon there, chatting about books and wandering the aisles. Then, I'll head to a nearby café to dive into my new treasure—it's the perfect Chelsea escape.

Favorite Pub — *The Avalon*

16 Balham Hill, SW12 9EB

The Avalon is a hidden oasis in the middle of South London. The garden is my absolute favorite—there's something about sitting under the fairy lights with a glass of wine that just melts the stress away. Inside, it's all about cozy sophistication, with leather chairs and a crackling fireplace in winter. I always end up staying longer than planned, splitting a bottle of something with friends and losing track of time.

Favorite Restaurant — *Rabbit*

172 King's Rd, SW3 4UP

Inventive, sustainable British food that doesn't take itself too seriously. Their farm-to-table approach means the dishes are always fresh and seasonal. The wild venison carpaccio is exquisite, and their sharing plates always feel like a bit of an adventure. The atmosphere is lively but intimate—perfect for a fun dinner that still feels a bit special.

What do you like most about living in London?

London feels like a living mood board—it's constantly inspiring me as a creative director. One day, I'll find a striking ad on the Tube; the next, I'm wandering through a tiny gallery that sparks a whole new idea. The city's contrast is what fuels me—chaotic streets like Oxford Circus remind me of the buzz of brainstorming sessions, while quiet corners in Chelsea feel like the perfect pause button. It's a city that feeds your creativity and never stops offering fresh perspectives."

Favorite Restaurant
— *Rabbit*

My secret to happiness:

"Pizza, pasta, and prosecco!"

Alessandra

Professor of Italian Literature

— Born in Florence, now in London, recommends...

🍴 Favorite Restaurant
— Napoli on the Road

9A Devonshire Rd, Chiswick, W4 2EU

Napoli on the Road brings the heart of Naples to Chiswick. Created by award-winning chef Michele Pascarella, it's no surprise the pizzas here are the stuff of lore. The Montanara, with its lightly fried dough, is pizza poetry, and their Diavola is perfectly balanced with just the right fiery kick. The atmosphere is warm and inviting, and you can taste the passion behind every dish. I come here when I've overdosed on London's amazing curry houses and craving a true taste of home.

Made or Born Londoner?

❝ *I moved here from Florence for a teaching position and stayed because I fell in love with the city's literary and cultural energy.* ❞

🔒 Secret Spot
— Chiswick Cinema

This independent cinema in Chiswick is modern yet intimate, with plush seating and a carefully curated selection of films—everything from art-house to classics. I love catching a matinee with a glass of wine and just getting lost in a good story. It's a space that feels like it was made for reflection and inspiration. Small independent cinemas are under threat from the plague of the multiplex, and it's these lone survivors like the Chiswick Cinema that have figured out how to stay relevant, while viable.

What do you like most about living in London?

❝ *London is steeped in history, yet constantly evolving. Walking through Bloomsbury and imagining the lives of writers like Virginia Woolf feels like stepping into the pages of a book. But what I love most is its mix of high culture and simple pleasures—like a night at the opera followed by a pint at a cozy pub.* ❞

🍷 Favorite Pub
— The George IV, Chiswick

185 High Rd, W4 2DR

The George IV is a Chiswick institution. I love the mix of old-world charm and lively atmosphere. It's my favorite spot to relax after lectures, especially on quiz nights, when the whole pub comes alive. Their wine selection is fantastic, but I'm partial to a good gin and tonic here. The garden in the back is perfect for sunny afternoons with friends, and their Sunday roast is genuinely the best I've found in all of London.

Made or Born Londoner?

> *I was born and raised in Bethnal Green—this place has always been home. Cockney London of the past has mostly migrated to the outer boroughs like Bromley and Havering, and Essex and Kent.*

What do you like most about living in London?

> *London's changed so much over the years, but the heart of it stays the same. I love the mix of old and new here—one moment you're walking past a skyscraper, and the next you're in a proper East End market like the one I used to go to with my mum.*

My secret to happiness:

"Never properly growing up."

🔒 Secret Spot
— *Mile End Park*

Mile End Park is a proper East End gem. It's got everything—canals, wildlife, and even a little climbing wall if you're feeling adventurous. I love walking through the Eco-Park area, where it's quiet enough to hear the birds and forget the city for a while. It's simple, unpretentious, and feels like home.

🍷 Favorite Pub
— *The Royal Oak*

73 Columbia Rd, E2 7RG

The Royal Oak is a proper East End pub. You walk in, and it feels like home—no pretension, just good pints and even better company. I've spent many a Sunday here after Columbia Road Flower Market, sharing a pint of pale ale and chatting with the locals. The old wooden interiors remind me of how pubs used to be, and their Scotch eggs are spot-on if you fancy a bite.

Terry Higgins

Retired Electrician

— Born and raised in London, recommends...

🍴 Favorite Restaurant
— *E. Pellicci*

332 Bethnal Green Rd, E2 0AG

E. Pellicci is a Bethnal Green institution. It's been here since 1900, and the warmth of the place hasn't changed a bit. Their fry-ups are unbeatable—crispy bacon, perfectly runny eggs, and proper thick toast. The staff know everyone by name, and the banter is as good as the food. It's the kind of place that feels like family, and there's nowhere better for a hearty meal.

Favorite Restaurant

— Govinda's Pure Vegetarian Restaurant

Made or Born Londoner?

> *I moved to London from Blackpool for film school, fell in love with its energy, and stayed to tell its stories through my lens."*

What do you like most about living in London?

> *London is a filmmaker's dream—it's raw, real, and always in motion. My first shoot here was in Brixton Market, and I remember being struck by the textures, the people, the stories in every corner. This city has an openness, a way of embracing all walks of life, and that keeps me inspired. Whether I'm scouting locations or just sitting on a bench with a coffee, there's always something that catches my eye."*

My secret to happiness:

"To surround myself with positive energy."

Amara Dhillon

Documentary Filmmaker

— Born in Blackpool, now based in London, recommends...

Favorite Pub
— The Montpelier

43 Choumert Rd, SE15 4AR

The Montpelier is one of those pubs that feels effortlessly cool. It's got a quirky charm, with mismatched furniture and a little cinema room tucked in the back—yes, an actual cinema! I came here for a pint once and ended up staying for a spontaneous film screening. Their burgers are great, and the atmosphere is always buzzing without feeling overwhelming.

Secret Spot
— Park Hill Park

Park Hill Park in Croydon is one of those places that surprises you. It's quiet and beautifully landscaped, with a little walled garden that feels like stepping into a secret retreat. There's also an outdoor amphitheater tucked away, which sometimes hosts small performances. I love coming here to think, plan a project, or just enjoy a moment of peace—it's a hidden slice of tranquility in the middle of the city with nary a tourist in sight.

 Favorite Restaurant
— Govinda's Pure Vegetarian Restaurant

9-10 Soho St, W1D 3DL0

Govinda's has been a little haven of calm in the middle of Soho since 1979. It's simple, wholesome, and feels like a home-cooked meal every time. Their thalis are my go-to—a perfect mix of fresh, flavorful curries, rice, and bread. The paneer tikka is incredible, and their mango lassi is a must. It's unpretentious, nourishing, and just the kind of food that makes you feel good from the inside out. Over 15,000 five star reviews on Google can't be wrong.

An interview with

Milly Kenny-Ryder

Food Writer, Potographer and Stylist

Milly Kenny-Ryder is a food and travel expert, specializing in uncovering London's culinary gems. Her work has been featured in publications like the Evening Standard and Conde Nast Traveller. You can follow Milly on Instagram @millykr and @weekendjournals.

How did you get started in food writing and blogging?

I started my blog when I left university fifteen years ago to document my favorite places to go and things to do. It allowed me to share my passions through a fun medium that was relatively new and exciting at the time, and became an online diary for me. At first, I wrote about anything that interested me, from art and fashion to theater and food. But once the aesthetics of photography came into the equation, I honed in on food and travel writing.

With the explosion of the food blogging industry, how do you manage to stand out and continue adding value?

I avoid trends and fads, and only post about experiences, restaurants, and dishes I genuinely care about. With the unpredictability of social media success, it's easy to feel tempted to post click-bait reels and TikTok clips, but it just doesn't interest me. So, I stick to things I know I am an expert in. If you have integrity, conviction, and vision, the content will appeal to the right audience.

What do you look for in a restaurant, bakery, or coffee shop to the extent that you would recommend them to your followers?

I care about a number of things; flavor and deliciousness are always paramount, but the story and the aesthetics behind a place also matter to me. Often, I'll follow a particular chef or baker's career, joyfully documenting their journey with my followers. I try to look beyond what everyone else is doing and discover new venues. It gets so boring seeing the same dish posted again, and again; I hope people come to me to discover something new.

In a highly competitive culinary landscape like London, how can an establishment make its mark?

London offers a plethora of options, so standing out is essential. However, innovation doesn't always mean avant-garde; the classic French bistro trend is thriving, offering comforting dishes at affordable prices. Yet, the true gems are those showcasing less common French delicacies like rabbit and île flottante.

How has the pandemic impacted London's food scene?

I think it is really suffering post-Covid, particularly with staffing, which is sad and is driving prices up, making eating out more of a luxury. I recently traveled to Texas and ate great BBQ and Mexican food. Neither

> # "I don't think we have enough chefs championing British food. It can be a fusion of cuisines and should be celebrated more."

cuisine is done that well in London (aside from Kol and Smokestak), but other minority cuisines, such as West African, are thriving, which is great to see.

What makes London's food scene unique or exciting compared to other major European cities like Paris, Rome, or Barcelona?

I believe London is currently leading the food scene. The variety and standard of fine dining, in particular, surpasses that of Paris and New York, in my opinion. We have numerous historic establishments that continue to impress, alongside a wealth of young, innovative talent showcasing food that demands attention, such as Ikoyi and Sollip. In essence, London restaurants exude more personality and are consequently more memorable. That said, I don't think we have enough chefs championing British food. It can be a fusion of various cuisines and should be celebrated more. I always recommend The Pie Room at Rosewood Hotel in Holborn for truly brilliant classic British homemade pies.

Do you enjoy cooking, and if so, what's your go-to, show-stopping pièce de resistance dish?

I love cooking but am rarely in for a mealtime. My biggest inspirations in the kitchen are my French grandmother and my dad, who can make a delicious meal from an empty fridge. My friends tell me my simple pasta tomato sauce is exceptional!

Do you have a bucket-list restaurant?

I'd love to try Alchemist in Copenhagen for its otherworldly experience and Sézanne in Tokyo for the perfect combination of French cookery and Japanese precision. I think I've tried every restaurant I want to in London—I eat out constantly!

Finally, if someone were spending just one day in London, what is the one food experience they absolutely can't miss, and what is the one thing that they must avoid at all costs?

Avoid the steakhouses in Leicester Square and head to the stunning Connaught Hotel for a meal at Hélène Darroze or Core by Clare Smyth.

Nosh like a native

Afters
Slang for dessert, commonly used in informal settings or pubs.

Bangers and Mash
Sausages served with mashed potatoes, often with onion gravy. A staple in traditional pubs.

Bottomless Brunch
A trend in London where brunch dishes are served with unlimited (bottomless) drinks, typically Prosecco or cocktails, for a set price.

Bubble and Squeak
A dish made from leftover vegetables (often potatoes and cabbage) fried together until crispy. Traditionally served as part of a full English breakfast.

Chippy
A colloquial term for a fish and chip shop.

Cockles and Whelks
Traditional seafood snacks, often served cold with vinegar, and associated with markets like Borough Market.

Cornish Pasty
A baked pastry filled with beef, potato, onion, and turnip (swede). Originating from Cornwall, it's a handheld meal historically made for miners.

Cream Tea
A simpler version of afternoon tea, featuring tea, scones, clotted cream, and jam.

Eton Mess
A dessert made of crushed meringue, strawberries, and whipped cream.

Full English (Breakfast)
A hearty breakfast including eggs, bacon, sausages, baked beans, tomatoes, mushrooms, and toast.

High Tea/Afternoon Tea
Afternoon tea includes tea, scones, clotted cream, and sandwiches. High tea refers to a more substantial evening meal.

Jacket Potato
A baked potato, typically served with toppings like beans, cheese, or tuna mayo.

London Particular
A traditional pea and ham soup, named after the thick fogs (or "pea-soupers") that used to envelop London.

Pie and Mash
A classic East End dish of meat pie, mashed potatoes, and parsley sauce (called liquor).

Ploughman's Lunch
A traditional pub lunch of bread, cheese, pickle, and often cold cuts or eggs.

Pimm's
A classic British summer cocktail with Pimm's No.1, lemonade, fruit, and mint.

Pudding
In British English, "pudding" often refers to dessert in general.

Sarnie/Butty/Bap
Colloquial terms for sandwiches, often referring to specific types like a "bacon butty."

Scotch Egg
A hard- or soft-boiled egg encased in sausage meat, coated in breadcrumbs, and deep-fried. Popular as a pub snack or picnic food.

Spotted Dick
A steamed suet pudding with dried fruits, traditionally served with custard.

Sticky Toffee Pudding
A dessert made with moist sponge cake, dates, and rich toffee sauce, often served with custard or ice cream.

Sunday Roast
A meal served on Sundays in pubs, featuring roasted meat, Yorkshire puddings, roasted potatoes, vegetables, and gravy.

Takeaway
British term for takeout food, often from casual eateries or delivery services.

Treacle Tart
A dessert made with shortcrust pastry and a filling of golden syrup, breadcrumbs, and lemon juice.

Welsh Rarebit
A rich, savory dish of melted cheese mixed with ale or mustard, served on toasted bread. Sometimes referred to humorously as "posh cheese on toast."

Yorkshire Pudding
A baked batter pudding traditionally served as part of a Sunday roast, especially with roast beef. Crispy on the outside and fluffy on the inside, it's perfect for soaking up gravy.

Booze like a Brit

Beer Garden
An outdoor seating area in a pub, often decorated with fairy lights and heaters.

Bitter
A traditional British beer style, pale in color and slightly hoppy.

BYOB
Bring Your Own Bottle; some pubs and restaurants allow this for a corkage fee.

Cask
A barrel of beer traditionally stored and served at cellar temperature.

Craft Beer
Modern, small-batch beers emphasizing unique flavors and brewing techniques.

Draught (Draft)
Beer served directly from a keg or cask, as opposed to bottled or canned.

Drayman
The person delivering barrels of beer to pubs.

Gastro Pub
A pub offering high-quality, restaurant-style food.

Guest Ale
Rotating ales offered alongside a pub's regular beer selection.

Half-Pint
A smaller serving of beer, often for sampling or a lighter drink.

Happy Hour
A period with discounted drink prices, more common in bars than traditional pubs.

House Pint
A pub's signature beer, often brewed locally or exclusively for the venue.

Landlord/Landlady
The person who runs the pub.

Lock-In
An unofficial practice where patrons stay in the pub after closing hours.

Pint
The standard unit for beer in the UK, equivalent to 568 milliliters.

Pork Scratchings
Crispy fried pork skin, a traditional pub snack.

Pub Grub
Casual food served in pubs, such as burgers, fish and chips, or pies.

Public Bar vs Lounge Bar
In older pubs, the public bar was casual, while the lounge bar was more refined.

Pump Clip
Decorative badge on a beer pump handle showing the beer name and style.

Real Ale
Traditional, unfiltered, and unpasteurized beer served from a cask.

Round
When one person buys drinks for the group, with turns taken to get the next round.

Session Beer
A low-alcohol beer designed for extended drinking sessions.

Shandy
A drink mixing beer with fizzy lemonade.

Snug
A small, cozy seating area in a pub, often with partitions for privacy.

Snakebite
A mix of lager and cider, sometimes with blackcurrant cordial.

Spirits Measure
Spirits like gin or whisky are measured in standardized pours, usually 25ml or 35ml.

Stout
A dark, rich beer, with Guinness being the most famous example.

Tab
Running a bill for drinks, more common in gastropubs or bars than traditional pubs.

The Local
A pub close to someone's home that they frequent regularly.

Directory by area

Pubs

Directory by cuisine

The Sunday Roast is more than just a meal; it's a British tradition steeped in history and family gatherings. It dates back to the early 15th century when the custom of roasting meat on a Sunday became popular among the working class.

— Central London

— East London

— Southeast London

100 LOCALS

Reveal their favorite local secrets

ABOUT THE 100 LOCALS SERIES

In this series of crowd-sourced guides of some of the world's most exciting cities, 100 locals share with you their secret spots, their top restaurants, and their favorite social hangouts such as bars, pubs, cafes, clubs, or nightclubs. Savvy travelers may already know some of these recommendations, but most are surprising additions you will be hard-pressed to find on the usual-suspect 'trip advisory' sites.

Packed with curated suggestions of where to hang out, eat, drink, and play in each city, this guide will prod you to venture beyond the epicenter of the metropolis to discover the best-hidden gems known only to the insiders.

The 100 locals are carefully selected to represent a wide cross section of each city's geographic areas, as well as a balanced demographic representation of gender, age, socioeconomic level, profession, and personality types.

Whether you are a seasoned traveler to the featured metropolis, a newbie, or indeed a local, prepare to take the express route to the very core that makes each of the cities in the series a unique destination to visit or live, and as far away as possible from the beaten paths and tourist traps.

Made in United States
North Haven, CT
09 February 2025